LIFE AND THOUGHT
IN THE ANCIENT WORLD

LIFE AND THOUGHT
IN THE
ANCIENT WORLD

by
C. CYRIL EASTWOOD

THE WESTMINSTER PRESS
PHILADELPHIA

LIBRARY OF CONGRESS CATALOG CARD NO. 65-21055

Published by The Westminster Press
Philadelphia, Pennsylvania

PRINTED IN THE UNITED STATES OF AMERICA

CONTENTS

PART I

ORIGINS OF RELIGIONS AND CIVILIZATIONS

PART II

HISTORY OF THE NEAR EAST AND THE
MEDITERRANEAN AREA

PART III

THE THOUGHT AND RELIGIONS OF THE ANCIENT WORLD

INTRODUCTION

The phrase 'the dead past' is a misnomer because we are continually being reminded that the insights and achievements of the past have shaped the present. The past lives in the present. No one can understand what a nation is today unless he knows something of its yesterday. But the past is not merely a distant static entity which we look at and appreciate, it is a dynamic influence actually shaping the religious, intellectual and social life of our time. Therefore, it is this sense of history which unlocks the meaning of the present. Modern Europe has been profoundly influenced by the religions, philosophies and cultures of the Middle East. The supreme factor in the story of civilization is the development of human thought. But it is important to understand how thought has been adapted to changing needs, and how sometimes these changing needs have prompted new thoughts and ideas which have resulted in new inventions and achievements.

There are two ways of approaching the subject of ancient life and thought: the first is to jump in at the deep end and this may result in panic, and the other is to wade around in water that is not too deep in order to get 'the feel of the thing.' A weighty volume which gives a detailed account of all the varied aspects of a nation's historical development is a formidable task as a starting-point. These chapters are to enable the student to wade around but they will only succeed in their purpose if they also prompt him to graduate to the deep end.

Moreover, in dealing with this subject it is a very good thing that the student should see the picture as a whole, to do this first, and then move on to an examination of the parts later. If one part interests him more than others he may well find that it will become a subject for further investigation, for he will have discovered where his real interest lies. By seeing the picture as a whole, he will appreciate the interaction between one civilization and another, the common elements in the social and political development of nations, the similarity of the religious conclusions reached by peoples widely separated in other respects, and the basic laws which have emerged almost inevitably in the development of all civilizations. It is precisely this 'sense of history' which will enable the student to understand, appreciate and interpret the world in which he lives.

For those who require a general introduction to ancient life and thought because it forms part of a specific course; for those who are interested in the question as to how man first turned his thoughts to God; for older students, no longer straining after examination rewards but anxious to expand and enrich their knowledge of a fascinating era in man's history, these chapters, it is hoped, will help and inspire. They are based on lectures given at a London University Extension Course for the Diploma in Biblical and Religious Studies, although the period covered by these lectures covers part of the course and not the whole.

PART I

CHAPTER I

THE ORIGIN AND DEVELOPMENT OF RELIGION

BEGINNINGS OF RELIGION

Is life complete with food and society? If man has sufficient food he can survive, and if he has company he can, to some extent, enjoy life. But is something else needed? Monkeys have few needs, they find their food easily and they like to live in groups. They need trees and other monkeys—this is a true summing up of their existence. But man requires something else. He requires culture. Culture consists of patterns or abstract ideas which are translated into concrete objects or actions. Having become aware of these patterns, man cannot ignore them. He accepts them as a way of understanding his whole universe. This has brought him his religion.

How does man face his problems? He meets some of them with real tools but even apes can be taught to use these. He meets other problems, like raising children and finding food, by certain practical rules. The fact that he also knows how to handle abstract ideas distinguishes him from the animal creation. For instance, an animal may be aware of what it is to be hungry or sick, whereas a man may be aware of what it is like to *foresee* being hungry or sick and to be apprehensive about it. In the awareness of such things as sickness and hunger mankind has been introduced to problems which cannot be attacked with spears, nor yet with regulations, but must be met with a third kind of resource— philosophy and religion.

What does man learn when he looks at the universe? He views it as the animals cannot and forms abstract ideas about it such as saying 'day' for the hours of light, and 'night' for the hours of darkness. He soon realises that the universe is not a tidy system, but he knows that while it has sufficient to look after him, it has many loose ends and many ugly gaps which somehow must be filled if he is to be safe. He knows that a hook and line will serve to close the gap between himself and food, and so satisfy hunger. The possession of a bow and arrow will help close the gap between himself and starvation. Of course, it is true that he must learn to use them but it is surprising how quickly a hungry man learns. He may also put an animal skin between himself

3

and the snow and this protects him from the biting cold. In all these things he learns to know and to use those things which are provided for him in the universe. But illness must be met with equal assurance, otherwise it will have a strong demoralizing influence on everyone.

How does primitive man face illness? First he symbolizes the cause of illness, and in his thinking, this must be either spirit possession or the effect of an evil charm. Then he symbolizes the cure: he takes a drink which the spirit will not like, or he uses a counter-charm which will break the spell and send the spirit back to its sender. Although this may seem to be a very primitive custom, in fact it represents an important step forward in the thinking of man. Let us notice what has happened: the situation had been put into a form in which it could be handled. The action may not work but that does not matter, because the main result is the completing of the system of ideas or symbols connected with the situation—the closing of the gap—so that anxiety may be allayed if not banished. This shows the symbolic nature of religion, for religion is much more than answers to problems, it is a way of putting the world into a shape which is comprehensible and satisfying. Man's mental advance makes religion, as the final appreciation of his world, not only possible but essential.

IDEALS IN STORIES

Religion and the supernatural are not necessarily the same. This is seen at once when we compare the story of the Good Samaritan with that of Little Red Riding Hood. The second is a folk-tale with a talking wolf, but it is not religious because it happens to be supernatural. The first story commands reverence and thought, and appeals to a deeper level in the mind.

General oral tradition is of immense importance in the development of man. It is true that sometimes the original message is lost on the journey, like the signal sent from Flanders in the First World War, 'Send reinforcements, we are going to advance,' which is said to have arrived at military headquarters as, 'Send three and fourpence, we are going to a dance.' But that is not the fate of every folk-tale, even though the imagination sometimes tends to obscure rather than explain the original truth. Folk-lore looms large among those who do not write their literature but keep it alive by telling it. Folk-tales are suitable subjects for what is now known as the process of de-mythologizing— that is, removing the trappings and trimmings in order to expose the original truth. When this is done it is possible to find the germ of an idea or, more likely, the suggestion of an ideal, in most folk-tales. It has sometimes been found that when the dust and grime, the paint and plaster have been removed from a church pillar, a good example of sculpture is revealed which was done several centuries earlier—perhaps the figure of a patriarch or an apostle. The same is true of folklore which may sometimes conceal a truth of permanent value.

When these stories reach us they may be a mixture of history and myth, or they may be just the result of pleasant romancing but even these may contain moral lessons. Even when they are myths of violence, and this is often the case, they may contain truths of value and the listener may form certain ethical ideas about them. If these myths only awaken dormant ideas or challenge the listener to further thought, they serve a useful purpose.

But sometimes they do more than this. Some of them are recognizably religious in character. The people of the Bakongo tribe in central Africa tell stories of Nzambi Mpungu (the supreme Being who made the world and punishes evil), and while they do not claim to know what he looks like or what his character is like, they have drawn some conclusions from the stories. They assume that there is a Creator whose demands are concerned with human conduct. They may still worship their ancestors, nevertheless great principles have been born in their minds.

Myths, therefore, are deeply sacred and are perpetuated by repetition and drama. They are means whereby people express many of their joint ideals. As the myths are retold, it is the moral values, so important to culture, which enable them to survive. People's myths are the main repository of their philosophy. If we define religion as 'the use of supernatural symbols or parables to fill out gaps in man's understanding of the universe,' then many myths should qualify as religious.

THE RELIGION OF THE HUNTERS

Bertrand Russell was once asked whether he thought the human race could survive, and he replied, 'Beyond all reason. I am unconquerably persuaded that it will.' Reason, however, played a very important part in man's early training. His mental faculties were developed by the way he faced and tackled his problems. The all-important question was: how to make an effective response to his surroundings?

One effective response was the making of tools. No doubt he soon realised that for felling trees, killing animals, and for building hunting stations, he needed tools. He made slow progress but the first man who stood with a stone chisel in his hand, having made it himself, marked an epoc in the development of our race.

Another important discovery soon followed, namely, that he could make a more effective response to his surroundings if some enterprises

were undertaken with the help of others. These communal under-
takings were especially necessary, for instance, in big game hunting,
and he depended on this for his food. Alone he was no match for animal
cunning, but in co-operation with others he had much greater success.
The emergence of the tribe or isolated group was no accident, indeed
survival and security were bound up with it. If he had to work together
with others it was important that he should be able to communicate with
them. Signs, symbols, and gestures followed by speech provide the
most significant development. Man's way of life was far inferior to his
capabilities until he learned to speak.

We may consider his hunting of the cave-bear and notice how his
response to his surroundings was accentuated by the demands of the
hunt. He could not afford to be daunted by failure. He needed tenacity
and intelligence in order to overcome many obstacles. He had to
outwit the animal he hunted; the animal had strength and an instinctive
sense of danger, but man had intelligence, and this together with
courage, eventually won the day. His intelligence and imagination
are also revealed by his choice of hunting stations and by the building
of gutters and fire-places.

He also sought in a crude fashion to satisfy his spiritual needs. After
the cave-bear had been caught, a prescribed ritual had to be followed.
After it was slain it was taken to a hunting station. The head was
treated with special honour: it was deposited in the interior of the cave
in an altar-like chest. Various undamaged long bones were hidden in the
cave in positions which made them a protection for the skull. The
centre of the ritual was the brain and marrow. These were offered to
the Divine Dispenser of hunting fortune as a token of thanks. This
part of the ceremony was carried out at the entrance to the cave which
meant that the deity was out in the universe beyond the cave. But
sometimes, even for the hunters, the deity was thought to dwell in the
bowels of the earth or at any rate in deep places. The fact that skeletons
of young does have been found in locks and pools means that the deity
was thought to dwell in the depths.

The hunters' magic was chiefly concerned with the animal which
provided him with food. Although it was his chief enemy, it was also
his staff of life. It was prepared to escape the hands of man by flight or
fight. Hunters and hunted belonged together. By imitating the animal,
man assumed its nature and life. Because he could lure and kill by
imitation, 'likeness' became the key to the mysterious power whereby
he could control other creatures.

Art, in so far as he had developed it, was used in the service of magic.
Magic did not engender art but it gave art its greatest scope and impetus.
Even this was part of their hunting ritual: they painted and engraved

in their caves and performed their mock fights and invocatory dances. Magic was also connected with maturity and the initiatory rites of the tribe's youthful members, and judging by the frequent occurrence of works of a sexual character, magic played an important part in the sphere of procreation. It should not be regarded as the product of eroticism but as the expression of a fundamental aspiration—human fertility.

THE RELIGION OF THE FARMING PEOPLES

There is no doubt that their occupation shaped their religion. The hunters had their distinctive ceremonies, so had the farmers. The numerous signs and symbols which have come down to us are connected with the cult of the sky and the sun. This is to be expected because the thoughts of the farming peoples were generally centred on the sun and the coming of the rains. Nature was their god because they were utterly dependent upon the powers of nature. Earth and sky, sun, rain and wind are the most important things for the tillers of the soil. The decorative motifs on their pottery indicate their religion. Doubtless some of the motifs are there for decoration only but many of the figures and symbols have a religious significance. For instance, circles, wheels and hooked crosses probably designated the sky, the sun and the earth. It is likely that the first two personified a sky-god.

If they were interested in nature, they were also interested in fertility. They developed the cult of the Earth Goddess and the Great Mother Goddess. For the most part the Goddess was a small image which was the result of their own crude workmanship. On special occasions the image was adorned with flowers and offerings of food were placed before it. The Goddess's male partner was usually in the form of a bull, hence the prominence of the bull in the art of the farming peoples. Various phallic rites and ritual nuptials were associated with it, for it was believed that in some way human fertility would be reflected in the fertility of their land.

Great reverence was accorded to the dead by the farming peoples. There was the preserving and painting of the skull which occupied a prominent place in the cave. The possession of the skull was regarded as a sign of protection, and always higher powers were ascribed to the dead than to the living. The tremendous efforts which they expended on the dead cannot be explained simply in terms of their concern for life beyond the grave. The explanation lies in the belief that the dead exercised some kind of power over the living and over the forces of nature.

They had their thanksgiving festivals which were observed in their own way. As we should expect, the burden of the farmers' entreaties to the heavenly powers, was the welfare of their crops, favourable weather, and a rich harvest. The sky or sun god is frequently represented as a spirit of fertility or a harvest god, and the people gathered before the picture or symbol of this deity to offer prayers and thanks. They also expressed their thanksgiving for the harvest by burying used sickle blades or stone axes in their fields. So the religion of the farming peoples may be summed up in the following way: their reverence for nature, their strict observance of fertility rites, the worship of their ancestors, alive or dead, and the various ways in which they expressed their thanksgiving to the deity.

CHAPTER II

ANIMISM

THE PRE-ANIMISTIC STAGE

(a) *A sense of Awe*. There is a Greek legend about a man who sat at the entrance to a cave. He dare not enter it because he was afraid of the dark, and he was afraid to move away because he heard the noise of thunder above and the growling of wild beasts around him. So he sat there hypnotised. We must not pretend that he rationalised his position or that he knew what we are now to say about him. In fact, he lacked two things: a sense of history and a plan for the future. He was afraid of the darkness behind him and afraid of the unknown in front of him. Since he was unable to draw any lessons from the past, he was also unable to look with confidence to the future.

Perhaps the sense of awe best expresses man's early emotions in relation to supernatural powers. The sounds that he heard generated fear. Storm and wind, thunder and sea instigated fear. But it was not only the noise that made him afraid, it was his inability to account for it. The silence after the storm was equally awesome, and this brought a sense of the incomprehensible. It was the same emotion which Wordsworth experienced on Westminster Bridge:

> *Dear God, the very houses seem asleep,*
> *And all that mighty heart is lying still.*

The ancient Egyptians worshipped a god named 'the Voiceless One,' and they believed that the millenium would be ushered in only when 'the Voiceless One' was heard to speak. In a desert land they had been impressed by the uncanny stillness of the endless desert.

Manifestations of great power also brought a sense of awe. The havoc wrought by a hurricane and the roaring torrents of a waterfall instilled into them a sense of fear of the things they saw but could not understand. Sight and sound and silence emphasized the mysterious element in the world in which they lived and their reaction is summed up in the phrase 'the sense of awe.'

It is important to notice that this sense of awe is present in all succeeding stages of religion, that it is the prime antecedent to the supernatural, and that the sense of wonder often turns into a sense of dependence. The belief in High Gods presupposes the feeling of the mysterious and awesome, and the latter was the first impulse to religion. This resulted in the consciousness of dependence on a supernatural power. Fear, wonder, and submission; where these are present there is the beginning of religion.

(b) *Fear and Awe*. Lucretius said that fear made the gods. There is truth in this statement but it is not the whole truth. Fear by itself makes for nothing but flight, but religion implies an approach to someone and not a retreat. It is only when fear is modified by other factors that either man or beast will turn towards, not away from, the object feared. So we come back again to the sense of awe which is a deeper and wider emotion than fear alone. Of course there is an element of fear in awe, but with it is mingled wonder, admiration, and self-abasement. Such a complex attitude is far more characteristic of religion than fear alone.

Again, fear tends to lessen with familiarity. If religion were solely a matter of fear, all that it would involve would be a means of providing escape from what is feared. When, for instance, there is a small-pox epidemic in a Dravidian village in South India, Poleramma, the goddess of small-pox will receive a great deal of attention and everything will be done to conciliate her as long as the epidemic lasts, but when the danger has passed, interest in the goddess will wane. Fear is present, but it comes and goes and it is not sufficient to hold the villagers' devotion permanently.

Further, primitive man was afraid of wild animals but his fear of them was very different from his fear of a ghost. He sees a wild animal and knows how to face it, but a ghost represents the supernatural and the unknown, and this inspires something deeper than fear. On the whole, it cannot be said that the crude emotion of fear alone accounts for religion.

The unusual arouses more interest and attention from man than does the usual. This applies to animals also. The regular sequences of nature are accepted but the irregular evoke strained attention mixed with fear. It is just because they are unusual that a shooting-star or an eclipse are greatly feared by people who do not know the cause of such phenomena.

But there is a deeper reason. Fear is usually due to the conflict between the desire to take action and the paralysing sense of ignorance of what action to take. In so far as the way of action is clear, fear is much less felt. What really affected man's attitude was not merely the awe-inspiring phenomena of nature but the idea of a potency manifested in them. 'Mana' has come to mean something that is of more than natural excellence or power. It is power or influence which is supernatural. This miraculous power is transmissable to things and persons, and accounts for whatever makes them in any sense extraordinary.

THE ANIMISTIC STAGE

Animism is the doctrine which places the source of mental or physical life in an energy which is independent of, or at least distinct from, the body. A distinction must be drawn between Animism and Fetishism. In the former it is the spirit which dwells in the object that is feared: in the latter the object itself is feared because supernatural powers are inherent in it.

Trees. The movement of a tree when swayed by the wind meant that it was a living thing or that it was animated by a spirit. The reasoning of primitive man was very down-to-earth and the theory of cause and effect was not known to him. As far as he was concerned, the movement of the leaves and branches of a tree denoted the presence of life. He believed that life was in the tree just as there was life in him. When he began to enquire how life could be manifested in a tree he drew the conclusion that it was due to the presence of a supernatural being. This being might dwell permanently in the tree or take up its abode there at certain times. To fell a tree, therefore, was a serious matter because a spirit was implanted in it. A tree was sometimes dedicated because it was believed that a spirit had chosen it as a shrine. If a supernatural being took up his abode in a tree, it is easy to believe that sometimes he would deliver oracles, and therefore the tree became more sacred still. Even to-day a water diviner will break a twig from a tree and this will help him to detect water, a sign of life, in some unlikely place. Does the twig possess supernatural power? Whatever the answer may be, a twig seems to be the indispensable equipment of the water diviner.

Streams and springs. Running water—rivers, streams, springs and wells, had activity enough to influence the thought of man, so these also were believed to be animated by a life and a will. Movement meant life, and because there was continuous movement in water this was sufficient evidence that it was alive. Man would also be impressed by the fact that its force and power were immeasurable. At first he thought the water itself was supernatural and later he believed that it was animated by a spirit dwelling in it. The Peruvians looked upon the ocean as a powerful goddess, and the Greeks had their oracle-giving springs which gave their message when a laurel leaf was dipped in them. The belief that supernatural beings dwelt in water persisted longer than the same belief in relation to trees, and there are two reasons for this: in many cases springs possessed minerals which had healing properties and this was thought to be a boon of the spirit which dwelt in the spring. Again, rivers and oceans were full of living things and it was believed that this was possible because of the living spirit which lived in the water.

Stones. Movement is not so obvious in regard to rocks and stones. Why then were these sometimes regarded as sacred? The reason is in their curious shapes rather than in movement. One rock may be balanced precariously on another, or a large stone may have the shape of a face, and such strange phenomena would be regarded with awe. In many cases these weirdly-shaped rocks and stones were made into divinities and prayers were made and gifts offered in front of them. A natural depression like a foot-print would inspire awe in primitive man. And as these rocks were often found on hills and mountains, the latter also were regarded as sacred.

THE POLYTHEISTIC STAGE

Let us state the *main reasons* for the emergence of Polytheism.

(*a*) Man faces many forces and not only one. He could not understand the possibility that the diverse supernatural powers in the world might have one focal point. As far as he was concerned, divine power was resolved into a sacred world of many potencies.

(*b*) In religions like Hinduism which accept the theory of innumerable avatars (incarnations), Polytheism inevitably arises. Any incarnation of Vishnu, whether in the form of man or animal or a combination of both, inevitably becomes deified. The idea, common to us, of a supreme revelation of God, is quite unthinkable in many parts of the world. And just because the race developed along the lines of tribe, clan, and caste, the fact is reflected in man's belief about the gods. The gods are often grouped together into hierarchies with an exalted one at the head of the Pantheon. Among people who had their own paramount chief the concept of a High God among many subordinate gods is simply the projection of a tribal belief into the realm of religion.

(*c*) 'Life like a dome of many-coloured glass
  Stains the white radiance of eternity.'
This idea may be true for us but primitive man did not think that life's many-sidedness was a stain upon eternity. Indeed he believed that no single image could tell the whole, and even though his gods and goddesses, his images and shrines, were but broken lights, they were a great help to him as windows to the eternal. To simple folk the many-coloured glass is a help not a hindrance. Hence the development of polytheism seems natural and reasonable.

(*d*) Moreover each god had his definite domain or sphere of activity. The encroachment of a god or even the approach of a devotee on the domain of another deity was an affront and quite often it was enough to start a tribal war. The Hebrews had no heart to sing the Lord's song in Babylon, and Naaman the Syrian was convinced that the rivers of his own city, Damascus, were better than all the waters of Israel. The villagers of South India are often very reluctant to leave the confines of their village, not because they are unattracted by fresh fields and pastures new, but because they are afraid to move beyond the sphere of influence of their god. Will he be able to protect them and assure them of prosperity if they are outside his sphere of influence? that is the supreme question.

(e) Legends surrounding village gods are manifold. Gods are brought into being to deal with a specific critical situation. Each god has a definite function and it is usually a function which cannot be fulfilled by another god. Many gods appear from a utilitarian motive. When the needs and tasks and desires and crises of the villagers are remembered, the multiplicity of gods required to supply these needs will be no surprise. During monsoon time when the river is in flood and the people afraid lest the whole village will be submerged, an old man is sitting in his bare mud-walled house. In his musings, he hears a voice saying, 'If you will build me a shrine at the end of the village, I will deliver you from the havoc of the flood waters.' He runs outside to tell the people this great news. But what form should the shrine take? Suddenly he sees a lime fruit on a lotus flower floating in the water, and it is clear that the Goddess of Floods should have a shrine in that form. It may well be that after a time the shrine will be neglected but it will always be remembered in time of flood and the name of the Goddess will remain.

(f) Sometimes one god will absorb the qualities of subordinate gods but the subordinate gods will continue to have an independent existence. For instance. Marduk is the solar god of Babylon, but Nergal is the Marduk of war, Enlil—the Marduk of sovereignty, Ninib—the Marduk of strength. So Marduk has the qualities of them all even though they remain independent and fulfil different functions. The Avatars of Vishnu have an independent existence also, but all are in some sense an incarnation of Vishnu. Such are some of the important reasons which led to the beliefs in many gods and goddesses.

It is sometimes supposed that primitive man's attitude to gods and goddesses was exactly the same as his attitude to evil spirits and demons. The belief in many gods has two points in common with the belief in demons and spirits: their multiplicity and the fact that they are unmoral.

The differences are striking. The first essential difference is that gods and goddesses have individuality and spirits and demons have not. It follows from this that gods and goddesses have names while spirits and demons have not. Again spirits and demons are not tied to a particular locality but gods and goddesses are. The former are sexless and are represented as hybrids or in the form of animals, while the latter are thought of as being human in form.

DEVELOPMENT OF IDOLATRY

The primitive worshipped idols because he was a Pantheist. If God was thought to dwell in everything, it was consistent to believe that He dwelt in some special object of their veneration. But he worshipped a stone image not because the object and the deity were one but because an outside spirit had taken up his residence in it. He did not worship the stone so much as the spirit in the stone. He worshipped a special stone image because that was the place where the spirit first appeared. From that moment the image received the homage of the people.

There were two time-honoured ways of dealing with spirits which he did not like: first by deceiving them, and this was done by placing cactus on the door of his house or outside his cave and this would convince the spirit that the house was deserted. Second, he would offer a propitiatory gift. He placed toddy (home-brewed beer) so that the spirit or demon would drink it and be satisfied. In any case the spirit would assume the place was deserted if the toddy was left untouched! Either way his method achieved its purpose. It is not suggested that these three stages—the pre-animistic, the animistic and the polytheistic—never overlap, but in general they represent man's early religious development. But it was not enough for man to know that spiritual powers existed, he was curious to know more about them and even to control and use them, so he turned to magic.

CHAPTER III

MAGIC AND RELIGION

THE BASIS OF MAGIC

Emotion. Magic is not always connected with evil. Indeed it is often connected with goodness and happiness. For instance, the magic wand transforms a situation, nearly always improving it. But magic is connected with the emotions and just because man feels before he thinks, magic precedes any advanced philosophy of life. To early man, magic was a supernatural energy inherent in the world. He was aware of it and made use of it long before he understood or explained it. Many have tried to explain it away, but it is a vain quest and would require a magician to do it. In any case, to shelve a problem is not to solve it.

The fact is that the primeval savage acted before he thought about his action. There was a stage of unreflective habits before ideas developed, and magic was one aspect of these habits. It is quite futile to attempt to introduce into magic things like ethics, ideas and ideals, because these have nothing to do with it. Magic is instinctive and emotional rather than rational. For instance, certain recurrent situations in social life induced a state of emotional intensity, and emotion must find a vent. So in time of tribal warfare, of funeral ceremonies and of pre-hunting rites the people would dress in leopard-skins, beat the drums and dance the dance of death. It is almost useless to try to explain these things, indeed all our explanations are but guesses. The only true way to understand them is to be identified with them. Beatlemania is akin to the primeval dance. The screaming of hysterical girls may not please everyone but in fact it is neither good nor bad, coldly interpreted it indicates an atmosphere, a feeling, and an experience for which no words can be found. The American girl who said when she saw the Beatles for the first time, 'I don't know how it is but they make me weep,' was no doubt telling the truth. Her emotions defied explanation. And if someone had told her that the Beatles had just landed from Saturn, she would most probably have believed it. For magic is often connected with emotional hysteria. The functionless and unaccountable activities of the Beatle fans are just as mysterious to them as they are to everyone else. If they cannot explain their actions, we have surely no right to expect the primeval savage to explain his. So he plays at dancing, hunting, fighting and love-making. He knows it accomplishes something but it is something he cannot define; it is magic.

Imitation. Primitive people commonly believed that their imitative characteristics had something to do with their efficacy. Just as a man who is shadow-boxing will imagine that the punch-ball is his next opponent, so primitive people anticipated the real occasion in their ritual dances. In fact their ritual was no more than the symbolic reproduction of their practical activity. This is explained, however, not by the philosophy that like produces like but by the vague notion that imitative practices exerted a sacred and powerful influence of the mana type. The savage comforts himself with no theory of *how* these ritual practices work, he is content to feel and know that they do work.

Incantation. It is interesting to notice that the action alone is rarely regarded as sufficient, it requires to be accomplished by a word or a phrase or even a verse if it is to be effective. This applies not only to early developments but to every form of religion. The Brahmins believe that the mantra or hymn gives efficacy to the sacrificial act without which it is valueless. The priest's duty in the Hebrew religion as well as in Brahminism was to see to it that the precise regulations were fulfilled and the proper words spoken. If the rules were not strictly applied the sacrifice was thought to be null and void.

For primitive tribes the intense feeling and the frenzied imitation are nothing without the incantation. Words always enter into it. The repetitive phrase, the slow incantation and the magical formula are essential and it is in these that the magical potency is believed to lie. Mantrams have such an influence over the gods that they are quite unable to resist doing anything either in heaven or on earth that the magician requires of them. Every other means remains ineffective until the magic formula is pronounced. These three stages, therefore, are indispensable: an emotional desire, a projection of the desire through imitation, and the fulfilment of the desire through the magical formula.

KINDS OF MAGIC

Simple magic. All of us accept sequences which we cannot explain. We dial a telephone number and we believe that there is a satisfactory explanation of how it works, and that given the right movements our connection will be secured. The fact remains that we don't quite know how it happens. Many of us accept a great deal of unscientific weather lore: red at night, shepherds delight; and if the morning is very bright we believe rain will follow. There may be something in all this but in any case we accept it without explanation. This kind of expectation that one thing follows another without any assignable reason is at the root of all magic.

Primitive people do not expect magic to do anything and everything, they use magic when their ordinary powers cannot help them. For instance, they do not use magic actually to catch fish, but they may use it before going fishing to draw fish into their nets or to multiply the number of fish in the water. They look to magic when their own abilities do not help them. This may seem irrational but there are occasions when it is social and cultural as well. It is not always done for private ends but sometimes for the common welfare. It is this 'public' magic which gives rise to the medicine man to whom the people will turn to find the cause of a general sickness, or a drought, or to catch an evildoer by divining. So there is a group dependence on magic and the result is often beneficial to the tribe. Of course in the light of advanced knowledge much of it seems no more than superstition, but for primitive people it was not necessarily evil, and often sustained them in their weakness and ignorance.

On other occasions they used magic to exert some special influence in a situation which was quite outside the normal and familiar sequences of experience. In some forms of magic coercion appears but not in all. The man who telephones does not try to *make* it work. If he fails, he assumes that there is something wrong with the works. This is very near to the primitive's idea of magic.

In the use of simple magic the magician is assisted by social opinion, suggestion, hypnotic influence and perhaps fear and fascination combined. At this stage the sheer power of imitation had not developed. Also at this stage magic was amoral, it was neither good nor evil, it was neutral. It was more a game than a serious pursuit.

Sympathetic magic. This stage is rather different; as in simple magic there is no evil intent and the aim is quite definitely constructive, but much more action and drama are involved. Magic helps to secure the survival of the tribe, to provide food, and to give protection. Garden magic, war magic, fishing magic, potmaking magic and love magic—all these are regarded as beneficial to the tribe. Here the power of imitation becomes more pronounced and this is illustrated by many forms of superstition. Animals express their desire by imitative processes. A dog fetches a ball and drops it at the feet of his master and at once adopts the position he had when starting to race for it. The desire is that the process will be repeated. A man rolls over like a wounded bear, and so illustrates his desire to be successful in the hunt. A man blows a conch-horn to bring wind, or throws water into the air to secure rain; he is acting his desire in a similar way to the animals. A row of girls sit on a log in a hut and go through the motions of rowing in order to ensure the safety of the men who are away on a voyage in rough seas.

The same law of sympathy applies to healing magic as well, except that the medicine man is usually an amateur psychologist also. He will apply his mouth to the site of the illness and suck, and in a few moments he will produce from his mouth a stone or a bone and claim that he has removed the trouble. The sense of relief that comes to the patient can be imagined. The main point is that he is doing something good and constructive and this is the characteristic of sympathetic magic. Of course this often appears to be no more than an imitative pantomime but the primitive's defence is that it works.

Sinister magic. Sinister magic is another term for sorcery. In its darker forms it represents evil and unsocial practices. An example of this is the Mass of St. Secaire. At 11 p.m. a bad priest comes to the ruined Church with his paramour as server and repeats the Mass backwards, finishing on the stroke of twelve. He is dressed in black and uses water from a well into which an unbaptized child has been thrown. The sign of the cross is made on the ground with the left foot and the man for whom the mass is said becomes ill and fades away. It will be seen that this is very different from the forms of simple and sympathetic magic which we have considered.

Three characteristics of sinister magic. (*a*) It is often hereditary even though it requires a certain apprenticeship and involves the magician in the rigorous tabus of his craft. Secret rites and spells and formulae are passed on from father to son, and the son swears on oath to keep the secrets and observe the necessary discipline.

(*b*) Its intention is always serious and sometimes evil. It refers to persons rather than events, and aims at gaining control over another person's desires and actions. The aim is the same as in brain-washing though the magician calls supernatural powers to his aid. It always contains an element of coercion. The sorcerer has one aim—to *make* his ritual and formula work. But it must always work against someone and never for them.

(*c*) Its aim is to coerce another person or a group of persons into an insoluble dilemma. It calls in good powers for an evil purpose. It does not ask which methods are right or wrong, it uses all means to accomplish its sinister ends. No one can say which came first—magic or religion, but it is very likely that the two attitudes were originally blended in a general attitude to supernaturalism.

WHY IS SORCERY ALLOWED TO CONTINUE?

Firstly, the sorcerer is greatly feared. He inspires a holy terror and generally people are afraid to disturb him in his dark preoccupations. In their minds he is associated with the most ghastly rites and ceremonies, and they believe he will not stop at murder. Fear makes people act irrationally. In normal circumstances, if they suspected crime, they would report it, but they are less eager to report a sorcerer. The reason is that they fear reprisals. It is said that folk in market places in African towns are usually very careful how they walk. They must avoid jolting anyone by the arm lest he be a wizard, and they will take the utmost care not to stumble over the pile of fruit on the ground lest a spell is cast upon them by an angry witch whose produce they may have ruined. So on the whole, they are over-anxious to be courteous but in their own interests.

The sorcerer is feared because his powers are invisible. Generally speaking people prefer to deal with the devil they know rather than the devil they do not know. In any case it is extremely difficult to tie the sorcerer down or to bring him to book. He operates in a realm where evidence is hard come by, and he is always particularly astute when his magic is needed in his own defence. Part of his craft is to learn to keep his own counsel and his own secrets. By remaining for the most part silent, he steers clear of trouble for himself, however much he may incur it upon others. He remains aloof even from his own colleagues for there is always the danger of retaliation, and there is no fury like the fury of a sorcerer offended by a counterpart. It is for this reason that he does not divulge to anyone what he is doing at any given time. He distrusts everyone and he works in the dark.

Moreover the sorcerer generally operates in remote places. In his haunts the laws of civilization rarely penetrate. He roams the woods, climbs the mountains, and spends weeks and weeks alone on the wind-swept moors. It is usually believed that the strange orgies of wizards and witches take place frequently but no one ever discovers their meeting place at the time. It is afterwards that the scene of their meeting is known, and then it is too late to take action because the law requires concrete evidence.

But the sorcerer has another great advantage which enables him to continue his dubious activities in relative peace. He always exercises remote control. Of course certain requirements are necessary to make this system function; for instance he needs a name, a talisman, perhaps even an image, but always a formula, but with this knowledge and equipment he seeks to wreak vengeance on his enemy many miles away. Who is to know the guilty party in these circumstances ? So the Law is baffled and the sorcerer marches on. These then are the reasons why sorcery is allowed to continue; it is not that the law permits it but that the law has little power to prevent it.

Perhaps a note should be added here about the modern witch. An attempt is now made to change the image of the traditional witch, and it is held that the present purpose of their secret conclaves is to face and overcome the world's problems, to restore broken relationships, to bring to bear supernatural powers upon the world's needs, to find new ways of healing. Indeed modern wizards and witches are bending over backwards to dispel any idea that they are sinister or malignat beings and to prove that their interest in human affairs is purely beneficent and good. Now all this may be so, but if it is, what is the necessity of doing these laudable things in secret? There is no need to conceal their good works if they are engaged, as they claim to be, in harmless philanthropic activities. Even so, if these are their declared aims, someone will have to find them a new name, because these enlightened aims are so out of harmony with the traditional interpretation of the functions of witches as to make the name 'witch' a complete misnomer.

MAGIC AND RELIGION

The limitation of natural powers. Magic, like religion and mana, often arises out of a sense of frustration. Man realises his inability to meet critical and inexplicable situations, and he does not know how to interpret the meaning of signs and wonders. Without thinking out his processes, primitive man manipulates his magic and uses his mana for specific purposes. The rain-maker, the seer, the diviner, and the spirit medium are all in some sense connected with magic. All are interested in supernatural powers; all wish to explore such powers, and all recognise how limited are their natural powers. They use other powers as the complement or completion of their own limited abilities.

Priests and magicians have certain things in common. Both are official representatives of others. Their office is sometimes hereditary, sometimes the result of special gifts, and sometimes it is the outcome of the will of the community. Both priests and magicians claim to be in touch with supernatural and transcendental powers. Such powers, in the case of magicians, may come to them from the spirits with whom they are in touch or through certain ecstatic visions, but in the case of priests these powers are bestowed either in a ceremony of initiation or through an outward act of ordination. It is necessary to make three qualifications, because it is unfair to state the comparison without showing the contrast: the priests receives a 'character' by ordination and this gives permanence to his office, whereas the magician or shaman tend sporadically to become spirit-possessed, and when a particular purpose is fulfilled he reverts to his normal state. Again the priest, at least in Christian thinking, claims to be in touch with the supreme God in Jesus Christ, whereas the magician makes contact with innumerable spirits of varying qualities and motives. Furthermore, the priest in fulfilling his true function, invokes spiritual powers for good and helpful purposes, whereas a magician may invoke such powers either for good or ill.

The control and use of supernatural powers. Magic is not easily distinguishable from religion but the fundamental distinction lies in the approach to and control of the supernatural order. On the whole, religion presupposes a reverential attitude and results in worship, humility and conciliation. Magic is essentially practical and consists in fulfilling prescribed ritual acts, and on the whole it results in fear and uncertainty rather than worship and conciliation. Whether or not spirits or ancestors or gods lurk in the background, magic always involves the knowledge and use of spells and formulae.

Magic usually stresses a non-human and strange order of reality. It uses supernatural powers to defy, dominate and destroy. This is not the purpose of religion. As it reaches out towards its highest expression, religion fosters the idea of fellowship and friendship in the universe, and it stresses how these are intended to help man. Magic hopes to make *some* things work together for man's good, religion hopes to make all things work together for his good. Consequently, it affords an inner sense of security, peace and well-being which magic cannot offer. But perhaps the ultimate and most important difference lies here: religion promises man its good through the goodwill of God, but magic offers to show man how to obtain certain things by his own endeavours. It follows that where religion is backward, magic lingers.

CHAPTER IV

TOTEMISM AND TABOO

ESSENTIALS OF TOTEMISM

Totemism means a form of society in which members of a clan or tribe believe themselves to be united by kinship to some animal or plant from which they are descended. It stems from the idea that there is a unity in the world of nature and that the life of man is inextricably bound up with the rest of creation. Closely associated with this idea is the concept of reverence for life which, in spite of clan, tribal and global war, has remained a permanent element in man's thinking. Mahatma Gandhi's doctrine of Ahimsa (i.e. non-violent non-co-operation) was based on the deeper and richer doctrine of reverence for all life. The same doctrine has inspired Albert Schweitzer and has been the spur to much of his social and medical work in Africa. But totemism is based on a reverence for life pact and this is something different from the doctrine of Gandhi and Schweitzer. In almost every case the totem is a friend and gives help, and it may be that because the totem is man's genial ally, beneficent and helpful in man's many enterprises, it has had such a prominent place in man's thinking and development.

The complete proof of totemism in any race involves the following points:

(a) The existence of tribes named after a plant or animal. Some of the animals chosen are: lion, ibex, wild cow, serpent, sheep, wolf, dog, panther and hyena. The list is given to show that man did not choose only those animals which were obviously friendly. Strength, cunning and swiftness are also represented in the list. The custom of naming a tribe after an animal has been prevalent in so many different countries that it cannot have been due to accident or metaphor.

(b) Ancestor worship cannot be separated from totemism, and one of the reasons why totemism is regarded as a benevolent institution is because the eponym animal (the animal that gives its name to the people) is also a tribal ancestor.

(c) The totem is nearly always regarded as sacred and this sometimes means that it is thought of as the god of the tribe. If we find all these things together in the same tribe, the proof of totemism is complete.

Kinship with the animal. It is recognised that members of the tribe are akin to the animal whose name they bear. For instance, the whole tribe mourns over a dead gazelle, and if a serpent is killed, all the members of the serpent clan are bound to avenge it. Coupled with this is the view that men can change themselves into animals. In South West Arabia it is believed that a party of men changed themselves into wolves in a time of drought, and the panthers of the Sinai peninsular are believed to have been men. Again, Muhammad would not eat lizards because he fancied they belonged to a matamorphosed clan of Israelites.

The totem animal was not eaten as ordinary food but it was eaten when sacrificed on special occasions. But of course this only applies to a tribe's attitude to its own totem. Obviously the attitude of outside tribes, whose totem it was not, was very different. At the same time, any tribe's totem animal is attacked at the peril of the attacker. A camel is sacred to the camel clan; locusts are not eaten by the Arabs, and doves are not eaten by the Syrians. This is entirely due to man's kinship with a sacred animal or bird. As a corollary of all this, sometimes an ancestor becomes a god. After the totem is selected it may eventually be recognised as being the form of a tribal ancestor, this in turn may be reverenced and worshipped as a god, so the development often follows this course—totem, ancestor, god.

The totem relationship. It should be remembered that the totem is related to every individual in the clan as well as to the clan as a whole. Although there is thought to be some link between the spirit of a departed member of the tribe and the totem animal, something more than a spiritual link with the past is envisaged. Often the relationship is thought to be one of kinship by blood. Normally the totem must not be destroyed. Members of the clan may not marry members of the same totem. Nearly always such ideas as heredity, exogamy and taboo are associated with the totem relationship.

Naturally there is a close association between the man and the animal whose name he bears, especially in those tribes where the name of the animal becomes part of a man's name as well. Hence there are the Kangaroo men and the Tiger men. In no circumstances will they harm the totem animal, and they will always defend it. It is also believed that sometimes these men take upon themselves some of the characteristics of the animals with which they are in affinity. Sight, strength, cunning and patience will be more fully developed in them than in others.

What is the origin of the totem? It is sometimes supposed that it happened by chance. Apparently certain tribes were given names and it was assumed that they were genetically associated with the creatures after which they were named. But such a facile explanation is discounted by the widespread occurrence of totemism.

Another reason that is often put forward is that totemism was planned in order to win the co-operation of the totem animal. The reason he chose a fierce animal was to ensure his own protection. Or was the totem animal decided by the locality in which the tribe lived? At any rate where a particular animal was found in abundance the word would soon go round that a nearby tribe was associated with that animal. It is said that Toda peoples treat their buffaloes as if they were members of the tribe—whispering secrets to them, giving them the pleasantest place to sleep, and garlanding them in a way they would not garland their own children.

IS TOTEMISM THE ORIGIN OF RELIGION?

It is thought to be connected with the idea of sacrifice. Alliance by means of a blood covenant was at the root of the idea of sacrifice. It will be seen that this is close to the totem idea. Originally the sacrificed animal was eaten by the worshippers and its blood was offered to them as a drink. This meant that the totem god and the clan were united. But with the decay of totemism, ritual killing fell into the background, and the eating of the animal gave place to a meal *with* the god, the food and fellowship being regarded as an offering to the god.

Not every sacrifice, however, must be regarded as having a totemistic origin. In order to clarify this point we shall describe the meaning of the Buffalo sacrifice in Dravidianism. The Buffalo is beheaded, its legs are cut off and placed in its mouth, and the fat from the abdomen is placed over its eyes. The legend behind this is as follows: A Brahmin had one daughter. A Pariah, disguised as a Brahmin, came to their home for tuition. The girl fell in love with him and they were married. She soon discovered that he was not a Brahmin but was warned not to reveal his low origin. The boy's mother who was supposed to be deaf and dumb, joined them, dressed as a Brahmin widow. In error one day the mother spoke. The daughter asked her father what he would do with a pot if he found a dog had licked it. He answered, "Throw the pot in the fire." The girl understood. She set fire to the house and burned herself to death. Her spirit appeared in the village, rebuked them for allowing her to marry a Pariah, and gave instructions for worship. Her husband was to be beheaded, his hands placed in his mouth, the fat of his abdomen placed on his eyes, and a light placed on his head in front of her. The Buffalo sacrifice was an enactment of the worship she had commanded, but there is no hint of totemistic origin here.

The Buffalo represents a fallen enemy. When the animal blinks in death a great shout goes up. The blinking of the eyes is regarded as the last act of submission of a conquered enemy. It is sometimes supposed that the hideous custom of wrapping the animal's entrails round the neck and taking its vitals into the mouth is an attempt to get into closer touch with the life of the totem animal. But this is due to a misconception. The point is that man tries to make himself as hideous as possible to frighten away demons. In any case the Buffalo is regarded as being ugly and vicious and this is not the kind of animal to become a totem. It appears from these arguments that the Buffalo sacrifice did not originate in totemism.

Another interpretation of totemism is that the totem is thought to be the receptacle in which a man kept his soul, or one of his souls. This theory succeeds in making a connection between totemism and animistic ideas, and it also explains the reluctance to kill the totem. It also suggests a reason for the connection between totemism and exogamy (marriage outside the clan). On the whole, however, there is not sufficient evidence to support the view that the totem embodied a man's soul.

It is sometimes argued that totemism was evolved as a system of magic whose purpose was to protect the tribe and to supply them with the commodities they needed. The churinga was something secret or sacred, and when an ancestor died the churinga was the receptacle of his spirit. The sacred stone was placed in a particular spot on the ground and was thereafter regarded as a shrine. This theory fails because the link between the churinga and the totem is not sufficiently clear.

Again there is the view that totemism is the symbol of man's religious consciousness, but this means that society equals god, and the whole issue becomes confused. The theory that animals were chosen rather than stars to symbolise man's religious consciousness because he was more familiar with animals is not very convincing. Therefore we conclude that the assumption that totemism is a trait in *all* primitive culture is untenable. It follows that the view that totemism is the origin of religion cannot be sustained, but it can justifiably be claimed that it is a phase in man's development.

THE ORIGIN OF TABOO

Is fear the origin of taboo? It is not easy to find a reasoned explanation for the existence of many taboos. The explanation seems less important than the fact and the customs which are associated with it. Taboo was often the most important factor in the life of the individual and the tribe. A breach of taboo carried with it the most fearful consequences. Why, then, were people afraid of taboo?

(*a*) Because it was possible for them to be tabooed without knowing it.

(*b*) Because taboo affected so many aspects of their lives: person name, food, property and tribe.

(*c*) Because the death penalty was sometimes the price of violating a taboo. This conviction was so powerful that sometimes a person would lie down and die, knowing that it was useless to fight against the consequences of such a breach.

Did taboo begin with royal command? Taboos often surrounded kings and chiefs and therefore it was assumed that those rulers had been responsible for instituting them. Can it fairly be maintained that taboos were enforced upon a tribe by its rulers? It seems unlikely for two reasons: firstly, it was in no sense a special honour to be associated with a taboo. On the contrary, it was a method by which the tribe was protected from the harm and suffering which might be imposed by the tabooed person. It is hardly likely that such a system would be instituted by kings and chiefs. In any case, taboo is far too deeply set in human nature for it to be the invention of rulers.

Secondly, the persons tabooed differed greatly in character and status. It is true that some were regarded as holy, but others were regarded as unclean and polluted. In their thinking no distinction was made between good and bad. The main point was that the tabooed person was thought to be dangerous and unpredictable. There were occasions when they were so dangerous as to be deified. This also was for the protection of the tribe. Perhaps the taboo was not thought to be effective enough and only deification would adequately protect them. For instance, some of the Hindu Sacktis were deified, not because they were holy and honoured (indeed some of them were regarded as immoral), but because they were terrible and unscrupulous, and therefore, the more to be feared.

Did taboo arise from religious tradition? It is sometimes supposed that particular religious observances might have hardened in taboos. The Australian Aboriginees usually associated their taboos with a totemic ancestor. The taboos connected with social laws, ceremonial practices and such customs as circumcision came from totemic ancestors. All the decorations of the body and ceremonial objects which are used in their corroborees are imitations of those originally used by the ancestor who instituted the rite. The taboos surrounding the rite as well as the rite itself go back to the original founder. This indicates that traditions sometimes become taboos. But this does not account for all taboos, for some of them are not connected with religion at all.

THE CHARACTERISTICS OF TABOO

Focus on the blood. The taboos associated with blood may be called the inherent taboos. Such taboos are particularly strong and are connected with birth, puberty and death. Certain actions, times and seasons may become taboo by association with something that is already taboo in itself. There is the law of uncleanness whereby accidental contact with blood or a corpse is an illustration of the contagion of taboo. The blood of Abel cries out from the ground and this is sufficient to put a curse upon Cain. David is forbidden to build the temple because he has been responsible for the shedding of blood.

Focus on the unfamiliar. Unfamiliar food, places or people were generally regarded as taboo. Those who had been in contact with strange tribes were often taboo. Strangers coming to the village were taboo. A census was forbidden because it involved asking for information which belonged only to the god. It was a short step from the unfamiliar to the sacred, and sacred persons and objects were always regarded as taboo.

Focus on the sacred. Consider the Ark of God. It contained the Covenant as well as other relics; it was a peculiar treasure of the Hebrews even though it seemed no more than a simple chest of wood, and its presence on the field of battle warranted victory. The association of the Ark with their wilderness wanderings made it even more important to them. But the Ark was taboo not simply because it contained sacred relics (the rod of Aaron, a pot of manna, and some stones of Sinai), or because it was a guarantee of victory in battle, it was taboo because it was the home of God.

The fact is that anything holy was dangerous to meddle with. Holiness meant unapproachableness, and the logical conclusion of this is reached when Uzzah inadvertently touched the Ark and fell dead in consequence. Whatever was holy was possessed of a mysterious and perilous potency and therefore it was wise to have as little to do with it as possible. The Sabbath was a holy day and some things were forbidden on the Sabbath; Sinai had to be approached with many precautions because it was a holy mountain; Moses had to remove his sandals because he was standing on holy ground. All this shows that sacred objects and sacred places were taboo.

THE CONSEQUENCES OF TABOO

That there are certain good consequences should not be overlooked. For instance, a Polynesian king had a given degree of mana, partly by practice and skill and partly by descent. This meant that the king had more mana than others. The king was taboo, and sometimes he was obliged to marry his own sister who was equally taboo. Yet it was this sort of taboo which gave to Polynesian society a strongly defined social structure. How important a part taboo has played in the sacred position of monarchies, it is hard to say, and although the position has been relaxed in recent years as far as some monarchies are concerned, it is true to say that for centuries the position of the monarch was secure because of the awe which surrounded the office. It was based on the assumption: "Others abide our question—Thou art free."

Further there is no doubt that the incest taboo has made for the stability of the family. Incest is considered horrible by all human societies, the exceptions permitting brother-sister marriage among kings do not count. This rejection of incest is certainly not due to instinct but to organized taboo. Here again taboo has been a blessing to the human race.

Again taboo has played an important part in awakening in man a sense of the holy and moving him to reverence. It is true that the higher forms of religion postulate something more than a defence-mechanism against danger, for it should become a positive experience of the love of God, but that the first is a phase in the process cannot be doubted. Fear and love always have their place in man's approach to God,

> It is my Maker, dare I stay,
> It is my Master, dare I turn away?

If love attracts, fear sometimes repels, and perhaps somewhere between the two is man's sense of 'the Presence.'

> Lord, teach us how to pray aright
> With reverence and with fear,
> Though dust and ashes in Thy sight,
> We may, we must draw near.

CHAPTER V

THE MEANING OF SACRIFICE

REASONS FOR SACRIFICE

Why was man first prompted to offer sacrifice? The short answer is that he was prompted to do something, anything, to indicate his feelings because he was not able properly to express them in words. Although this is true, it is an over-simplification. The story of man's reactions and responses to external stimuli is a very complex one. When a baby is confronted with a steam engine, he blows out his cheeks as if he considers it quite incredible that a thing so huge should exist. If he is confronted with a pretty doll, a benign smile crosses his face and he gently strokes the doll, at least showing that he is not afraid of it. If he is shown food, he will clap his hands, lick his lips and make all sorts of pleasant noises. If he is taken to church, he will move his head in this direction and that as if he is not sure where to focus his eyes. In fact the child has shown fear, pleasure and wonder according to the various kinds of phenomena which he has seen. The child, of course, does not understand what has taken place, and even if he knows that the objects he has seen are different, he does not ask why. His reactions are quite spontaneous, they are not necessarily rational. Now substitute primitive man for the baby, and just because he is placed in a strange and wonderful world which he does not understand, it is very likely that his reactions will be very similar to those of the child. He could not comprehend the world in which he found himself. He saw the earth and the sky, he saw that certain objects were still and others mobile, he heard sounds and wondered, he saw death and trembled, he hungered and suffered, but he did not initially ask 'why,' he simply felt and acted. It would have been as natural for him to have asked 'why not,' for his actions were first instinctive, then rational. The more childlike the idea of God formed by primitive man, the more natural and easy was for him the introduction of sacrifice.

MEANING OF SACRIFICE

Was sacrifice purely and simply an offering to God? In answering this, three points should be borne in mind:

29

(a) Man's motives are instinctive before they are reasoned. His first instinct may well have been to give something away, whereas after he had rationalised the matter, his attitude might have changed.

(b) To provide food is a sign of friendship, and it is obvious that man intended the gift to be a sign of goodwill.

(c) In any case, a really primitive race has little else to offer in the way of gifts.

The aim behind the gift is almost always conciliatory—the attempt to be on friendly terms. It cannot be denied that there was also the expectation of benefits to be received: "Here is butter, give us cows."

But if all that signifies a sacrifice *to* the god, there is also another idea which implies the sacrifice *of* the god. This means that the sacrifice is slain, not as a victim, but as the representative of the god. It is sometimes held that sacrifice develops out of totemism and that the essence of it is communion. The eating of the totem becomes the act of union between the totem and the human clan. At any rate the idea of a common meal has usually been regarded as a means of establishing unity.

However, other interpretations have been put forward. One of these is that the shedding of blood or the taking of life is in order to transmit prosperity and fertility. For instance, the killing of a young king was to ensure while he was still young that his power and fertility would be conveyed to others. On this view sacrifice means the giving of life to promote and conserve life.

But sometimes sacrifice is thought of as a medium of communication. It is intended to establish through the victim a communication between the sacred and the profane world. The sacred is generally identified with mana and is therefore taboo. But sacrifice offers a means of getting in communication with the sacred. Preparatory rites are observed in order to make the offerer, priest, and victim, fit to enter into relationship with the world of the sacred.

We should not imagine, however, that only one motive underlies all forms. The earlier notion, the idea of getting into a right relation with the gods through the offering of something which was pleasing to them, was not lost in later forms.

The Homage Theory. To this must be added what is known as the Homage Theory. Although man did not know what to make of supernatural powers, it is curious to note that he allowed himself to be bound hand and foot by them. He did not know what to believe about 'the Wholly Other,' yet he had no desire to escape from it. If he could not understand these supernatural powers, he could at least indicate his submission to them. Therefore, his first act of worship was probably a symbol of his dependence upon God. Without considering the meaning of sacrifice, or its utilitarian value, or the question of its results, man sacrificed. This was his symbol before his language became so. When we speak to a friend we cannot thrust our meanings directly into his mind, we can only come as far as the frontier and signal our meaning, in the hope that he will interpret the signals correctly. If sacrifice was a signal of man's submission to God, it was not revealed to him that his signal was misplaced. For instance, "Abel brought of the firstlings of his flock and the Lord had respect unto Abel and to his offerings."

The Gift Theory. The Gift Theory has received strong support for three reasons: because it is possible for man to make a gift even though he may not be aware of the motives and reasons behind it. Secondly, inasmuch as the offerings were often only food and drink, the issue was not confused by the idea of propitiation which is bound to arise when blood sacrifices are included. Moreover it was generally believed that material gifts were pleasing to the god who received them. But two problems remain: we may wonder whether primitive man was quite as altruistic as this theory supposes. Was he really so ready to give up to the divinity some portion of his possessions? Such an idea seems to imply a sort of instinctive generosity which is not quite in harmony with all we know about man's selfish nature. In any case, food and drink may be properly regarded as offerings but they cannot very well be regarded as sacrifices, so the theory is defective for that reason too.

The Common Meal. The idea of sacrifice as a common meal has become complicated because of its association with totemistic theories. If pressed this theory implies that the divine dwelt in the totem animal, and that by eating the animal man assimilated the divine life. It was this assumption which drove Freud to the noxious conclusion that therein lies the explanation of the Christian Eucharist. The common meal theory is hard to justify because there is no trace of totemism in the practices of certain races. Even where it does exist it does not belong to the earliest culture. If we take the classification primitive, primary and secondary culture, we should have to place totemism in the secondary category. In any case, sacrifice was not always accompanied by a meal so the theory breaks down at this point also.

One reason for preferring the homage theory is that it stands firm even though we do not know the nature of those mysterious powers which man sought to approach. What was the character of those supernatural powers which seemed to be related to man's life and welfare in a strange but vital sense? Were they good or evil, friendly or hostile, beneficent or cruel? The fact is: we do not know. Nor do we need to know, for we can accept the homage theory irrespective of the answers to those questions.

Man sought communion with those powers not out of a sense of guilt, but rather out of a desire to express his sense of dependence on them. To give expression to these sentiments he fell back on a language which is more powerful than speech, the language of action. To primitive people there came thoughts of one who was ruling them as they ruled the sheep, who in some strange way made the seeds grow which they put into the ground. How should they please him and manifest their subjection? Speech and thanksgiving are not the most childlike ways of expressing homage; acts go before words. Primitive man was in no sense inhibited in his actions, his thought was directly converted into the deed. In fact it may be claimed that very often the deed was the substitute for the thought. It is for such reasons that the homage theory is preferred to the other two.

THE GOD WHO SEES

It is important to notice the influence of the 'eye' in primitive thought. There is only one thing worse than the knowledge that a microphone is hidden in the wall, and that is the feeling of being watched. Man has always had the uncomfortable feeling that someone is watching his actions. If he acted cruelly or wickedly he knew that his actions were noticed. Of course this had a salutary effect in curbing evil and imposing restraints. And in earliest times fear was as good a check as anything else, but it could not remain so. It was soon realised that factors other than fear prompted man's actions. At the same time he realised that if he acted nobly, his action was seen. "The eye of the Lord is upon them that fear Him."

But the fear of the eye began with the tribal chief before it was related to the tribal god. The chief of the tribe might listen to the words of his people and also speak with them, but it was neither his tongue nor his ear that they feared. They feared his eye. But if sometimes the eye of the chief was upon them in anger, it was also upon them in blessing. Now the primary demand of the chief was obedience and loyalty, and the best way to demonstrate that loyalty was by deed rather than by word. It is relatively easy for a man to swear loyalty to the death for his chief's sake, but it is a very different thing when a man falls upon his spear in the presence of the chief to show and prove his loyalty. By this the chief knows that a man's obedience has turned into sacrifice and this is the sort of devotion the chief understands. It is not enough for him to hear of it, he must see it.

The chief would sit in front of his tent in the evening and see the gifts of his people placed before him. These were a sign of respect, a sign that they acknowledged him as their chief. Of course there were times when such offerings were personal gifts and could not be regarded as the recognition of the chief's authority, but the chief would rarely receive these things as personal gifts. For instance, the mirasdar in an

Indian village will acknowledge but will not touch the gift brought him by the villagers, and this is not due to the caste barrier. The truth is that the mirasdar does not need the gift but he is glad that it is offered, so he merely smiles in acknowledgment. If the chief and the mirasdar are pleased, it is not so much with the gift as with the demonstration of homage and obedience which the gift reveals.

In some religions we find that it is essential for the Swami to see blood. At Kaikalathur in South India the villagers worship Kaliaman. They will kill a goat in the presence of the Swami, then drag it round the shrine three times. After this process, blood will flow round all the shrine. The Pujari will not drink any of this blood (as is the case in some ceremonies), nor will the blood be poured into a coconut shell and given to the local washerman (as in others), it will merely flow round the Swami's shrine. The villagers believe that the Swami must *see* the blood, she sees it and is satisfied. The blood must be brought as visibly near to the goddess as possible. Whitehead has pointed out that sometimes a curtain is drawn in front of the Swami in order that she may not see the shedding of blood. But this is not the case unless that particular goddess does not appreciate blood offerings, and there are very few, if any, Dravidian goddesses who do not desire blood offerings. If two shrines are close together and one Swami desires blood offerings and the other does not (for instance, a Hindu shrine and a Dravidian shrine in close proximity), then a covering may be put over the Swami who is offended by blood. But there is no case where a Swami who is satisfied by blood is shielded from seeing the sacrifice.

THE GOD WHO DEMANDS

There is at present a considerable revolt against a god who demands anything. Man doesn't want a god who is authoritarian, strict and righteous, but one who is kind, indulgent and useless. But this is partly due to modern man's preoccupation with self, and to his sophisticated view of his own importance. In this respect he has something to learn from primitive man. For primitive man could not stand the idea of a feeble god; he cried out for demonstrations of power, strength and authority. A god who demanded nothing was not worth having, a god who could be ignored was a god who could be discarded.

A discussion has been going on for a long time as to whether we should believe in a God who demands or a God who offers, and almost every time the victory goes to those who support the second. In fact, there never were more ridiculous alternatives. It is rather like the Chinese legend of the witch who was thrown into the river in order to find out whether she was innocent or guilty. If she floated, she was proved guilty and was taken away to be burnt; if she sank, she was proved innocent but was drowned nevertheless! She had no choice, poor thing, and neither have we. The offer we shall consider later, the demand is unmistakable. It was early recognized that from man's hunting and harvesting God demanded a share. The first-fruits were brought to a shrine. The first-fruits included the first-born of the family, the first-born of the flocks and the first-fruits of the field. This was not only recognizing the divine demand but also the priority of it. Man's duty was to set aside something for God because He demanded it. And this brings us to one of the basic truths behind sacrifice.

(a) *The claim to ownership.* God is the Owner of all things. The act of creation is also the claim to possession. Such a claim is clear in Ps. 50 "Every beast of the forest is mine, and the cattle upon a thousand hills. I know all the fowls of the mountains, and the wild beasts of the field are Mine." This therefore is the reason why the first-born of all the cattle and fowls ought to be given to God: it is the recognition of His ownership. It is natural that the three feasts which every Jew was directed to observe were connected with agriculture. The first was the Feast of Unleavened Bread. It occurred at the time when they "put the sickle to the standing corn" (Deut. 16: 9); it synchronised with the first cutting of the barley—the earliest crop—and the people were enjoined to bring "the sheaf of the first-fruits of their harvest" to God for an offering (Lev. 23: 9). The second was the Feast of Weeks, which came seven weeks after the first barley harvest. This took place at the end of the reaping season when all the wheat and barley had been cut and gathered, and marked specially the termination of the wheat harvest. The third was the Feast of Tabernacles—the Jewish Harvest Festival, celebrated when all the harvest of fruit, oil and wine had been gathered in. All three festivals were thus connected with harvests of one kind or another, and at all three the Israelites were to make their thank-offerings to God in recognition of the fact that all the produce of the land was a bounty from the hands of God Himself and that he was entitled to such an acknowledgment of the fact.

(b) *The Bread of God.* The early Hebrew sacrifice was a clan-feast in which the worshippers had festive communion with each other and their God. The idea of a meal dominated the ritual and the usual accompaniments of the meal were bread, wine, oil and salt. These were known as the bread of God, and the altar on which He accepted them, was His table. The burnt offering often accompanied the meal and drink offerings. The way in which such offerings were accepted by God is typified in the Bible from the story of Noah's sacrifice after the flood which the Lord smelled as a sweet savour to the reference to the offering of Christ as the "odour of a sweet smell" (Eph. 5: 2). But if these early offerings were known as the bread of God, they throw an interesting sidelight on the significance of sacrifice from the divine angle. They were not merely expressions of man's gratitude, for they were essential, not simply desirable, to God Himself.

(c) *The Communication of Life.* There was always the underlying assumption that nothing was quite as efficacious as blood. The blood enabled life to be shared and this was true of the ritual of the tribe even before it was applied to religion. So the idea of the sharing of a common life appears in the Arab phrase "our blood has been shed" meaning the blood of an individual. And if this holds good in the life of the community, it may also apply to their relationship with God. So we must not forget the basic aim of sacrifices: to establish union between man and God and to restore that union when it has been broken. Although the ritual varies with different sacrifices, the result was the same: hostility was minimised, favour secured and a bond of unity established. To make this effective three principles had to be observed: the offerer had to be identified with the victim. This process of identification was symbolised by the fact that the offerer had the courage to draw near to the altar and lay his hands on the victim. The second principle is this: it was necessary for something to be forfeited or destroyed in order to establish a right relationship with a transcendent source of strength. Something must be sacrificed if life is to be released. Here again the emphasis is on the giving of life to promote and preserve life. Nevertheless the destruction of the victim is incidental to the liberation of life and power inherent in the object sacrificed. The central point is not the slaughter but the application of the blood and the sharing in the life.

A word should be added about the custom of child sacrifice. There is no doubt that it was prevalent in Palestine before the Israelite occupation and probably continued until the exile. It was regarded as a tribute to God for the use of fertile soil. It is likely that the first-born of the flocks and herds were substituted for the first-born children but this would take place over a long period and is mistakenly attributed to story of the proposed sacrifice of Isaac. It is reading too much into the story to say that God was teaching Israel that human sacrifice was not required. The story illustrates a test of obedience, and when God was satisfied that Abraham stood up to the test, there was no point in carrying it to its logical conclusion. The story of Jephthah's vow shows that the custom was still accepted in Israel, and the castigations of the prophets against the cultus were no doubt prompted by their repugnance of child sacrifice.

THE GOD WHO GIVES

There is one sentence in the story of Abraham and Isaac which will always throw light on later events. To Isaac's question: "Where is the lamb for the burnt offering?" Abraham replies: "God will provide Himself a lamb." It was a deeper insight and not merely a brighter dream that God himself would provide a sacrifice which would render all other sacrifices redundant. But man had first to realise that he was dealing not only with a God who sees and demands but also with a God who gives. The new truth which was revealed was that God loved freely and unconditionally. The essence of the Christian Gospel is summed up in the words: "God so loved. . . that He gave." The bargain basis is gone, and God is seen as no respecter of persons. He makes the rain to fall on the just and the unjust and offers forgiveness without charge, He Himself having paid the price. His gifts are not offered according to man's deserts for, as the Parable says: "When they had nothing to give, He forgave them both." He gives continuously lest anyone should think that His loving nature changes. Now all this is part of Christ's legacy to the world. These truths about the character of God and His plan for mankind are made known in Christ. But they present one important problem: in what terms can they be understood by man?

Both in recognizing God's gifts and in receiving them man has no alternative but to resort to symbols. All the time man is trying to give outward significance to truths which are just beyond his grasp. So he becomes essentially a sacramentalist because in relation to spiritual truth he is bound to be. For instance, a man is knighted by a specific ceremony: he kneels under a sword, makes an oath of allegiance and is endowed with the appropriate insignia. In the same way a ring symbolizes the life-long vows of marriage. Patriotism is symbolized by a national emblem. A badge or a ring or a flag may or may not be of very great intrinsic worth, but their significance lies in the intangible loyalties and mysterious powers which they represent. If the sacramental principle is necessary in man's relationship with man, how much more is it necessary in man's relationship with God.

Consequently the great acts of God are represented under visible signs and symbols. So Baptism by immersion symbolizes the completeness of man's redemption. It means the end of the old life and the beginning of the new, the transition from death to life. The Lord's Supper symbolizes the event by which man is redeemed. It implies the dramatic identification of the believer with the Death and Victory of Christ. The Gospel itself symbolizes the love of God in action in the life and teaching, the Death and Resurrection of the Redeemer. The Church symbolizes the community of the redeemed, and worship is man's response to the self-sacrificing God. Sacraments, therefore, are man's attempts to understand sacrifice from the divine standpoint as well as from his own. The two cannot be separated, for since no man has seen God at any time, there is no alternative but to worship Him under temporal conditions and by signs and symbols. Sacrifice is turned into sacrament so that man might understand spiritual truths and receive spiritual power.

CHAPTER VI

THE HOPE OF IMMORTALITY

MAN'S PERENNIAL HOPE

Man has entertained this hope for a very long time; he hopes he is immortal, and that is a fact. No one will doubt the existence of the hope but whether it can be substantiated is a different matter. Some dismiss the hope altogether as an illusion. They will not believe it because they cannot be absolutely certain about it. Of course if a man could be absolutely certain about it, there would be no need for him to believe it. Perhaps it should be said at the outset that absolute certainty eludes us on most subjects, if not all. It is hard to imagine any truth which is so utterly demonstrable that it leaves no room for doubt or enquiry. Perhaps we were never meant to be absolutely certain, and since this would require absolute knowledge of all the facts, it is doubtful whether we ever shall be. But this does not preclude moral certainty. In this case, doubts, problems and mysteries remain, but they call forth enquiry and investigation and the highest ventures of the human spirit. If a man says that he will accept nothing but absolute certainty, then the argument is closed. But he will be closing his mind not only against the tenets of religion, but against everything else as well.

Others may say that the hope of immortality is unnecessary. They consider that it undermines the meaning and reality of earthly life. If a man has this life only, he is likely to put more into it and live more fully, than would be the case if he had the promise of a life beyond this. Yet a man who believes in the life beyond does not necessarily belittle earthly life. On the contrary, he may consider that a life that is endowed with eternal values is altogether more significant than a life which is confined to temporal ones.

THE REASONS BEHIND THE HOPE

At any rate, there are several broad reasons why man has always concerned himself with immortality. He does not easily accept the fact of death. The one certain thing about earthly life is that it must end. Over all his plans and enterprises there looms the shadow of death. Death is life's greatest mystery. Other mysteries he can deal with, but

this one baffles him. It involves a complete break with life as he understands it; it is unpredictable, impenetrable and final. When he asks
questions about life he is also asking questions about death. What is
life? What is man? What is truth? What is goodness?—all these
questions can be put in a different way. For instance, is life simply a
number of years? Is man mortal or immortal? Is there such a thing as
eternal truth? and is there such a thing as absolute goodness, and if so,
where is this to be found?

In seeking to answer these questions man's actions have been even
more important than his words. Elaborate burial rites have been
practised by all races and in all ages. Man's farewell to earth has always
been accompanied by elaborate preparations for something else. The
idea of a journey is prominent. Socrates prayed that his journey to the
gods might be prosperous. Death appears to mark not the end of a
journey but the continuance of one. This may account for the presence
of food vessels, personal belongings, sword and shield in many ancient
tombs. Clearly it was thought that these things would be useful in the
continuance of the journey. The words "Go forth upon thy journey O
Christian soul," so often spoken at Christian funerals, corroborate these
ancient burial rites.

In addition to this there is the persistance of the conviction at least
among primitive tribes that the spirits of the dead possess far greater
power than the spirits of the living. This phenomenon is not solely
due to fear because in those races where ancestor worship is highly
developed, it is strongly associated with the veneration of the spirits
of ancestors and not fear of them.

In many religions there is the recurrent theme of the dying and
rising god. It is true that this refers to gods and not to men but it must
be remembered that men have perpetuated the belief and it may be
based on the quite reasonable assumption that there is little hope for
man's immortality if the gods do not rise again. Here again there is the
strong protest against the idea that death is the end.

Nor must we forget the practice of prayer in all religions. It is not
suggested that prayer means the same thing for people of all faiths yet
some aspects of prayer appear to be common to all people. For instance,
generation after generation have believed that powers exist which are
not subject to the laws of mortality. What is so often overlooked is that
the answer to any prayer involves an element of miracle. The miracle
must take place in and for human lives. Now all this presupposes a
relation between the natural and the supernatural, the mortal and the
immortal. As long as man continues to pray, he is indicating that he is
not out of his depth when he is in touch with immortal powers. This
fact suggests that man is not entirely bound by the limits of mortality.

Man is often aware of hopes and dreams which are too sublime to find their fulfilment on earth. Of course he dreams of a perfect world in the sense of an earthly utopia, but on the whole his sense of destiny transcends earthly life if only because his dreams of a perfect world do not seem to materialise here. Is such a dream due to dissatisfaction with the present world? Is it merely the refuge of the frustrated and the disillusioned? Is it due to the fear of complete oblivion? Or is it merely the hope of a recompence after the set-backs and sufferings of earth? A perfect world implies a sphere in which perfect bliss is possible. But such an ideal cannot be realised in a world of time. We know that the earth and material things will eventually pass away, and if the ideal is real, it must be looked for outside the sphere of the material world. It appears, then, that man's *home* is in that which is unseen and abiding. While rejecting the Platonic theory that man *has* a soul, we claim that man *is* a soul in the making. Buddha envisaged a state of existence in which there would be no suffering; the Persians looked forward to a day when the age-long conflict between Ahura and Arihman would come to an end and peace ensue; the Hindus look to the time when the Atman will be united to Brahma and this will result in perfect bliss; the Hebrews look with eager eyes for the coming of the Day of the Lord:

> The day in whose clear shining light
> All wrong shall stand revealed,
> When justice shall be clothed with might,
> And every hurt be healed.

If it is asked whether such hopes can be realised on earth, the answer is that such is man's perennial hope. Beyond all reason he still waits for the dawning of the Day of God here. But if amid the changes of this mortal life man looks forward with such confidence to such a day, it is surely not unreasonable for him to look for it beyond the limits of his earthly life. It is just as likely, perhaps even more likely, to find fulfilment there as here.

Alongside all these hopes and aspirations there is the universal desire for salvation, and whether he thinks of salvation as deliverance from time, from earthly existence, or from evil, the hope and desire remain constant. Salvation is often understood as perfect freedom, and if man holds the strong conviction that such freedom is only possible when he is freed from the bonds of mortality, he may be equally convinced that his hopes are not misplaced.

THE ELEMENT OF HOPE IN RELIGION

The nature of hope differs widely. Sometimes it is confined to this life and is thought of only in terms of earthly prosperity. He hopes for success in the enterprises undertaken, for victory over his enemies, for fertile fields and abundant harvests, for many children and for health and strength and many days.

Sometimes the social aspects of hope are more prominent, like the messianic expectation of Israel. The centre of interest here is the state rather than the individual, and the future to which they look forward is a renewed and re-established state.

At other times this hope refers to the deeper needs of the spirit. The deliverance man seeks is release from inward conflict, for this alone will bring inner harmony. He may feel that the span of life is too narrow to offer the fulfilment for which he craves. He is all the time looking for "Life's wider sphere and its busier enterprise," and feels cribbed and cabined within a sphere which only partly fulfils his truest desires.

> Let no man think that sudden, in a minute,
> All is accomplished and the work is done;
> Though with thine earliest dawn thou shouldst begin it,
> Scarce were it ended in thy setting sun.

So he continues to look for further opportunities and new experiences in a different sphere.

But sometimes, like the Buddhist, he seeks rest rather than continued activity. Away from the succession of desires, disappointments and failures, he hopes for peace. If the Buddhist is asked what reason there is for believing that the future can furnish what the past has failed to provide, he will reply that self-renunciation, not self-expression, is the path of peace. What is needed for the soul's salvation is not deliverance from individual desires, but from desire itself. What is needed, he will say, is that utter passivity which is found in the dreamless sleep of Nirvana.

THE ELEMENT OF FEAR

No race holds that death is complete extinction. But it must be admitted that very often fear is the spur to man's hope. There is the fear of the unknown. We view the unknown with fear chiefly because it is unknown. What is known is no longer quite so fearsome to us. Such fear is usually born of ignorance and lack of experience, and a fuller knowledge helps to dispel it. Nevertheless fear has taught man many lessons. It serves not only as a warning against danger but also as a challenge. Acts of heroism, courage and self-sacrifice are undoubted signs that fears can be overcome. In the end, the question arises as to whether there are qualities which are greater than fear. Where love, trust and a spirit of endurance are present, fear takes a second place. It is true that these are supernatural qualities, yet they are often revealed in human lives. And just because they supersede fear, they also help man to face death unafraid. It is the presence of such qualities which strengthens our hope of immortality.

THE ELEMENT OF MEMORY

There are strong arguments for immortality in the phenomena of dreams. When the images of persons whom he knows to be dead appear to a man in his dreams, he naturally infers that these persons exist somewhere and somehow apart from their bodies. How could he see dead people, he asks, if they did not exist.

Memory plays an important part in many tribal ceremonies. An attempt is made to recapture the past, and such a vivid impression is made on the mind that people are convinced that the past is being re-lived. It is not unusual for members of the tribe to believe that those taking part in the ceremony embody the spirits of those long dead. Again, resemblances which children bear to their deceased kinsfolk appear to have prompted in the minds of primitive peoples the notion that the souls of their dead ancestors have been re-born in their descendants. All this has strengthened man's belief in survival, and although there is much that remains mysterious, the occurrence of strange dreams, vivid memories, and striking resemblances, has helped man to draw his own conclusions about this important matter.

THE ELEMENT OF THE FAMILY

It is impossible to omit a consideration of ancestor-worship and the cult of the dead. Primitive people were extremely demonstrative in everything and especially in their demonstrations of grief at the death of a relative. Perhaps this is why some of them hired professional mourners. Their loud weeping and wailing was supposed to show the deep regard for their deceased relative. While demonstrations of affection, grief and the desire for reunion with the departed do not amount to ancestor worship, they certainly indicate the process by which ancestor worship developed.

The first condition of any such development is that the expressions of grief should harden into custom. When these ceremonies at death have become conventional expressions of grief, it becomes possible for fear to operate. There is the fear that something maybe overlooked and the conventions not properly observed. Fear, as we have discovered, is an element in reverence, and the omission of any part of the pre-scribed ceremony might imply dishonour and irreverence. When it was thought that some of the conventions had been neglected, further rituals had to be undertaken and the ceremonies became more and more elaborate. Something had to be done to please the dead. Offerings of food, hair and blood were made to the dead, and although these customs may now seem strange to us, they indicate man's belief in survival.

But in time these gifts constituted a kind of worship. Such worship was the responsibility of the family as a whole. Prayers were said, gifts were offered, and the virtues of the departed one were extolled. In this way ancestor worship was established as a private cult.

THE ELEMENT OF DEIFICATION

From all this three important developments took place. In many cases superhuman powers were ascribed to the spirits of the dead. We have already seen that these spirits were thought to be more powerful than the spirits of the living. Nevertheless it was widely held that those spiritual powers could only be used by the living. One of the reasons why these rites were strictly observed by the family was to prevent any human gaining power over their dead. It is in this sense that it is sometimes said that the ancestor is dependent on the descendant.

All the same, it is true to say that the ancestors were sometimes raised to the status of a god, but this does not prove that the gods to whose rank the spirit was promoted, were originally ghosts. What, then, are these gods? The worshipper's pride was that *his* ancestor was a god and no mere mortal. Ancestors known to have been human were not usually worshipped as gods, and ancestors worshipped as gods were believed not to have been human. Of course this gave some scope to the imagination, and there is no doubt that some ancestors were invented in order to enhance the family honour.

But ancestor worship was never the only worship of the tribe. Wherever it is found it exists side by side with the public worship of the gods of the community. The two systems seem to have developed together and the one form of worship was strengthened by the other. The present insistence on a decent interval between death and burial, burial in consecrated ground, and gifts of flowers, is not all that far removed from some of the customs of primitive people.

THE STATE OF THE DEAD

The element of judgment is more or less a later development. Primitive people believed that the progress and bliss of departed spirits depended to a great extent upon the living. The fears were not directly connected with the welfare of the dead, they were sure that everything would be all right if the family played its part faithfully. Their greatest fear was lest anything should be left undone.

The dead were thought to dwell in the underworld, but the underworld was thought to be cold and cheerless for everyone. Sometimes the dead were thought to dwell in some distant region of the earth. Although the dead were far away, it was generally assumed that they were safe. Another view was that the spirits of the dead inhabited a place in the sky. In fact, the Greek word 'ouranos' which we translate heaven means 'aerial regions.' Of course there are those who believe that the spirits of the dead have no static abode, but that spirits are reincarnated in the lives of their descendants. Sometimes the spirits are thought to wait in the grave until a child of the same tribe is born. The more elaborate transmigration theory offers the spirit no rest. On this theory the spirit passes from one body to another for there can be no such thing as a disembodied spirit.

Our main concern here has been to indicate man's early strivings as he faced the fact of death. We have considered the matter entirely apart from the truths embodied in the Christian Faith. We have dealt with hints and suggestions, but we may be surprised at the strength of the case for man's immortality even without the Christian revelation. Nevertheless it must be said that the coming of Christ introduced an entirely new dimension into man's thinking on this theme. We no longer rely on vague intuitions or what have been called 'intimations of immortality,' we have certain objective facts on which to base our case. In Christ the Eternal has entered into the temporal, and the event of Christ's life and death and resurrection has given us an assurance that was not otherwise possible. He has dealt once for all with man's greatest enemies—sin, guilt, death and annihilation. His own experience of life is the first fact: He became man. His teaching that man's true nature is to be a child of God is the second fact. His Resurrection which made this possible is the third fact. His life, his teaching, his Death and Resurrection, these are facts based on historical events. The whole tenor of His teaching assumed that man may share in an eternal destiny. One sentence of His has been sufficient to dispel many doubts and to give reasonable grounds for hope: "I am the Resurrection and the Life: he that believeth on Me, though he die, yet shall he live." This sentence, confirmed by the manner of His own death and its victory has done more than anything else to reassure his followers. This sentence has changed man's attitude to death as well as to life. Christianity, therefore, affirms that there is no situation in which the Christian cannot find meaning and hope, and to this, death is no exception. Stated simply, the Christian case is that man finds fellowship with God here in this world, and it is a fellowship which nothing has the power to destroy.

CHAPTER VII

THE SEARCH FOR POWER

MAN'S FEAR OF THE POWERS OF NATURE

Man is a fearful creature. His basic fear is of the unknown. He is afraid because he does not understand. Primitive man was afraid of the unknown and this fear has lingered because of his inability to penetrate the unknown. He fears death because it is an unknown experience. He is not only afraid of the things which may hurt him, he is afraid of the things which mystify him. He is even more afraid of annihilation. He is afraid of death not only because he loves life but because he loves power and yearns for knowledge. Man is essentially an explorer. He loves to explore the regions of the mind and spirit as well as the unknown regions of the world in which he lives.

Primitive man was convinced that the powers of nature were hostile, therefore he was afraid. He was afraid of fire, drought, and wild animals because these had the power to destroy him. He assumed that they were controlled by higher powers which he did not understand. It was for this reason that the Aryans in their early gropings after God, worshipped Agni—a terrestrial priestly deity who was depicted as the sacrificial flame carrying the worshippers' prayers to the bright heaven. Agni was fire and this conception always remained in close connection with the flame that burned the wood upon the altar. But fire and light banish darkness and so in the Rigveda men pray:

> *Chasing with light our sin away, O Agni,*
> *Shine thou wealth on us;*
> *May his light chase our sin away.*

The Hebrews thought along similar lines. God appeared to Moses in the bush that burned and was not consumed. The true God was the one who answered by fire on Mount Carmel. The altar fires were kept burning continually. Although they did not know it, perhaps God was helping them to overcome their fear.

Men were afraid of drought because their very existence depended upon the fruitfulness of the land. The Aryans worshipped Dyaus Pitar 'Heaven Father' who appeared in company with Privithi, the Earth Mother, as a personification of the sky, fructifying the earth with life-giving rain. The Psalmist was sure that Someone had power over

drought and this helped to dispel his fear. He spoke of the God. . .
"Who covereth the heavens with clouds, who prepareth rain for the
earth, who maketh grass to grow upon the mountains."

They were afraid of the ferocious animals which roamed the impenetrable jungle. How small man seemed when compared with these
monsters. The Aryans worshipped Indra, the warrior god who slew
demons, men, and animals and showed forth his inconquerable power.
For the Hebrews God was the victor over Leviathan and over all the
monsters of the deep. Those who trusted God would stop the mouths
of lions and tread on scorpions without hurt.

To be sure in earliest times they feared the forces of nature but they
found great comfort and strength in the thought that someone had
power over the forces of nature. This realisation was a great step
forward but much more was to follow.

MAN'S VICTORY OVER THE POWERS OF NATURE

God has given man three important gifts: a mind, an artistic sense, and
a capacity for hardship and heroic endurance. Without these gifts he
would not have been able to survive. When he was faced with a problem
he could ponder it in his mind, when he saw beauty he was able to
appreciate it, and when he was faced with an important task he was
able to face it with courage and hope.

The problems which confronted him seemed less formidable when
his mind was brought to bear upon them. Man cannot solve all the
world's problems but he can name them. He cannot reach the stars
but he knows their number and name. He had named the mountains
and seas of the moon long before any missile had reached it from this
planet. All great revelations and revolutions begin in the mind. Once man
realized that he had a mind as well as an arm, he began to make progress.
He had noticed that many things were provided by the good earth: fruit
and nuts in the jungle, and here and there a spring of water on the
green hill side. If he found wild figs in the jungle, perhaps if he planted
a seed he might grow them himself. If he found perennial springs on
the hill side, perhaps he may find hidden springs on the seemingly arid
plains, and if he did, the problem of drought would be partly solved.
Further, if he grew crops and fruits in abundance he might store some
of them, so that when the rains failed, he would not starve because he
had something stored away in the barn. When he had learned to sow
and reap, to harvest his crops and irrigate his land, man had made his
first outstanding discovery—the secret of the land. This was the beginning of agriculture.

Then he had to find means of carrying water for his own use and he also needed something in which to store the grain and keep it dry. He knew that clay was pliable and could be pressed into different shapes and he also knew that it hardened under the heat of the sun. So he hit upon the idea of making earthen vessels. If he could make one, he could make another. The second one might be more beautiful. In this way he made his second great discovery—how to make pottery.

Yet he knew that compared with some of the mammoth creatures in the jungle he was very small and weak. There were great slabs of solid rock which he could not move. There was a limit to the amount he could carry from the fields to the barn. He could not run fast enough to catch the swift deer. He might make some of the stronger animals help him in these tasks if he could tame them. In this way he reached a third and vital stage in his development—the domestication of animals.

Now let us notice what he has done. Having overcome his fear of fire, drought and animals, he has controlled these erstwhile hostile forces and used them for his own purposes. Hence man's three earliest conquests and the beginning of civilization as we know it—agriculture, pottery and the domestication of animals. By using God's gifts of mind, aesthetic sense and capacity for endurance and courage, man has worked a revolution which has redounded to his benefit and happiness. But much has happened, for in the process he has become conscious of himself and his own powers. He is no longer obsessed with the idea of size. He knows that size is no test of importance. The smallest ant on the mountain side is much bigger in the order of creation than the great mountain on which it lives, because the ant is alive and the mountain is not. Nor is man any longer obsessed with the fear of wild animals for he has gained dominion over them. We have seen men who have kept a tiger in a cage, but we have never seen a tiger which kept a man in a cage. We could not view such a contingency without alarm and this would not be simply for the sake of our own skins but because it would imply a major reversal of nature, it would mean that brute force had overcome the power of the human mind. It is always difficult for man to keep a balance between achievement and responsibility. When he seeks power for power's sake without any sense of responsibility or justice, he becomes a tyrant. His greatest problem is to curb ambition and to find his true place in the universe. He goes wrong when he seeks to control other men's minds, destroy their lives, and abuse the gifts of mind and spirit with which he has been endowed. He must recognize the limits of human power.

> *There are two laws . . .*
> *Law for man and law for thing,*
> *The first builds town and fleet,*
> *But it runs wild, and doth the man unking.*

The world is intended to be his home, but what is a home like if servants become tyrants, if children become traitors and men become monsters?

DIVINE AND HUMAN POWER

The development of man may be viewed in three separate ages: the Age of the Land, the Age of the Machine, and the Age of Power. In the first, man's concern was food. Physical survival was the only aim he knew. His principal demands were at the physical level and he was able to deal with them.

Man has to live not only as an individual but as a community and he can only do this if he is able to compete with other nations in the markets of the world. Hence there dawned the Age of the Machine and with it came a sense of security and prosperity. Just as man was able to cope with the problem of the land, so he was able to cope with the machine age.

Now there has dawned the Age of Nuclear Power. What will he do? Our contention is that the instinct of self-preservation, human in-genuity and technical skill will not now suffice. He will need more than these to face the complexities of the new age. He has reached an impasse. In facing this problem it is important to bear in mind three great truths: that all power belongs to God, that the value which God has placed upon human life has not changed, and that God's unique power is always the power to redeem.

God and man never meet on equal terms. There is no question of balance of power in this relationship. It is to misunderstand the whole situation merely to hope that this new power may be dedicated to God. It *is* God's. It is not God's rival but His agent. And it is not new for it originates in God. Each new discovery is, in fact, a discovery of divine power. Each discovery tells us more of God. The real question is not whether God's world is safe in man's hands but whether it is safe in God's. Man possesses delegated power, power as a trust and not as a right. With all his dark conspiracies and evil tendencies, he has no power save that which is given him from above. Sometimes he forgets this but he does not forget with impunity.

The greatest victories in this world have been won by spiritual means and this is a fact which no discovery or achievement can change. We may mention but a few examples: the open sepulchre, the beginnings of Christianity, the continued expansion of the Church, the changed face of many nations, the spiritual harvest of over fifty million people in half a century, the incomparable power of the Word of God and the evidence of the operation of the Holy Spirit in the world. The man who seeks to explain away these facts will be explaining away human history. All of it has been wrought by the power of God.

If man is now faced with a gigantic problem and if sometimes he considers it insoluble, it is time he sacrificed his pride and asked, Insoluble to whom ? The words of Whittier ring true.

Who fathoms the eternal thought ?
Who talks of scheme and plan ?
The Lord is God, He needeth not
The poor device of man.

Man's bewilderment must be viewed in the light of God's wisdom, and man's impotence in the light of God's power. The world is under rule but it is God's rule. No man will ever be the arbiter of the destiny of the world. The sole Ruler is God. This is a function which is unshared. Man is permitted to know and do in this world as much as God sanctions. God sets the limits to man's knowledge and actions, not man. The history of God's dealings with man shows that He has infinite trust in man. This clearly involves risk.

But man, proud man, dressed in a little brief authority,
Plays such fantastic tricks before high heaven
As make the angels weep.

All this is permissible; what is not permissible is that man's fantastic tricks should determine the destiny of the world or flout in the long-run God's good purpose. Yet the evidence of history is that a false word or a hasty action or a foolish command may bring irreparable harm to mankind. So man is always hoping that his own folly will not cause him to miss his providential way. Meanwhile it comforts him to know that in the Mind that rules there are no problems unsolved, no purposes unfulfilled, no future crises unforeseen, and most important of all, no evil unatoned.

The value which God has placed upon human life has not changed. Every new discovery enriches and enlarges our conception of the character of God. It is equally true that every new discovery increases our moral and spiritual responsibility. The truth is: man is now more dependent upon God, not less. His fundamental needs have not changed, neither has God's capacity to supply them. In every age God hands to man a new key so that he may unlock the door to greater wonders. The key to an understanding of immeasurable power has been given in our time. It is unthinkable that it should not sometime be given. Does this mean that man is now good enough to handle this new gift ? Certainly not. Man is never good enough to handle God's great gifts. God does not wait till man is good enough. That is the essence of grace. God gives in love and expects man to receive in faith. This is the gist of the whole matter: he finds an answer to the age of the land and to the age of the machine but he has no human answer to the age of power apart from God. What man needs over and above everything else is the power to do God's will. Weakness at this point is weakness everywhere. Man can only handle this immense gift under God's grace. Knowledge and Grace must go hand in hand.

At the same time there is one power which God retains—it is the power to redeem. This is His prerogative and can never belong to man. Above everything else our world needs redemption. Redemption is in God's power only. As Augustine said, "God is always active and always at rest." How true this is! Always active because everything must be brought into subjection to Him; always at rest because the ultimate outcome is known. The Gospel is the Power of God unto salvation and that is enough for the Christian. He may not always understand, he may frequently fail, but his faith will not let him relinquish his hold on the supreme truth that all power belongs to God.

CHAPTER VIII

THE SOCIAL FUNCTION OF RELIGION

LAWS WITHIN THE GROUP

What are the reasons for the continued existence of the Group? People are always ready to form an organisation. Interestingly enough the groups persist even when the objects for which they were formed have lost their value. People who are members of a tribe, a social or religious group, or a political party, keep on holding together even after the purpose which originally united them seems to have vanished. Although they may forget the reason which brought them together, they do not lose the vitality which continues to integrate them into social unities. A procession will pick up followers, not because they are particularly interested in a cause but because they want to be with others. The Toc H survives even though many of its present members knew nothing of the Flanders battlefield, and perhaps have never really known the purpose for which the Toc H was formed.

Moreover a group is instinctively antagonistic towards those who threaten its existence. Civilized society cannot stand thieves or men of violence. Dishonesty and violence are repudiated more by instinct than by intelligence. It is not so much the common judgment as to what is wicked as the common instinctive sense as to what is fatal to social life which leads to the elimination of violence. There are other crimes which are equally violent but there is no common mind about them. The instinct of preserving society works with tremendous power. This is true of animal life also. An elephant which becomes violent is instantly turned out of the herd. The herd must be safeguarded at all costs. There is a modern counterpart to this aspect of group life. A man is sent to Coventry because he has broken Trade Union rules. He may not have committed a serious crime but he has done something of which the group as a whole disapproves. It is this jealous guarding of group life which has played an important part in its survival.

Laws have emerged from social groups. The contact of man with man is different from the contact of man with things or even with animals. In this area too we find that man is constantly at work in search of unity. It is in the development of law that we see most clearly man's striving after unity. Tribal law is usually no more than case-law: a number of decisions are handed down from the chieftains of the past, guarded in the memory of the elders of the tribe, and applied with greater or less success to any new cases which may happen to crop up. This body of traditional law or lore is quite unsystematized. Some of these case-laws may turn into no more than traditional taboos or mere tribal prejudices, but others develop into moral codes of behaviour. When these laws come to be regarded as *moral* codes which must be obeyed, we are very near the meaning of religion.

LAWS BEYOND THE GROUP LIFE

Man is conscious of laws that he did not invent. When he has made laws himself he knows something about the way they work. But there are laws operating in the world over which he has no control. Eventually he comes to realize that he has no power over them. He learns to accept them, but he does more: he associates them with the supernatural and places them in a separate category. This body of supernatural laws may be described as Providence. We should not forget that all through the human story there have been three vital concerns: the protection of the tribe, the propagation of life and the production of food. Where laws operate and further these ends, man has considered them good. There has been provided wild honey for food, herbs for healing, sunshine and rain for his crops, the river to water his lands—and all this is not of man's contriving. Even when these laws have worked against his interests, he has regarded them with reverence and awe rather than with rebellion. When he began to recognize the laws which he had not made, he was on the threshold of religion.

THE BASIS OF SOCIETY

The aboriginal has a deep sense of the sacred and the eternal. To him the universe is alive, and nothing that lives ever really dies. Usually he believes that man is essentially spirit, and sometimes he believes in re-incarnation. He is not greatly interested in cosmology; he takes the world for granted but he peoples it with living beings everywhere. All life is one and because this is so, he believes it is possible through prayers and ceremonies to move the sources of life. Between man and some natural object there may be a definite relationship or kinship and this is always characterized by mutual sympathy, dependence and helpfulness. For instance, the totem creature and the native are one and the same thing like a man and his photograph. Almost all ceremonial practices and social laws come from totemic ancestors. The succession reaches a long way back, but it is a unity in depth as well as in length.

Now this process has had two important results—the survival of the tribe and its solidarity. So intimate is the association between the totem and the totemite that the blood-relationship means the sharing in a life-principle, making all members of the same group one flesh. Since it is the duty of each clan in this primitive co-operative system to ensure the fertility of its own totem plant or animal by the performance of the prescribed rites, it has also ensured the survival of the tribe. The tribe has also enabled its own sacred species to multiply since its members were forbidden to eat an animal with which they were in a sacred alliance. Of course, the attitude of one tribe to another tribe's totem is entirely different, nevertheless the system as a whole has preserved society.

It follows that society was consolidated and unified as a social organism on the basis of its unity with the supernatural source of its life. Each totemic unit has made an independent contribution to the renewal of vitality for the entire community. There is little doubt, therefore, that totemism, once established, exercised a powerful influence on the social, economic and religious constitution of society.

THE BASIS OF CULTURE

Culture is the human contribution to the world. It consists of all the traditions, inventions and conventions ever made by humanity. Let us contrast man's behaviour with that of a chimpanzee. The actions of the chimp are purely repetitive, it makes no progress. Every band of chimps behaves in the same way: the same in their manner of eating, in sleeping in nests, in jumping around and making a noise. All this is characteristic of the chimps and it is determined by their general nature and capabilities. The case of man is different: although in some ways he is repetitive, he is also an innovator. Not only has he the ability to adapt himself to his surroundings, he adapts his surroundings to his needs. He does not walk to the river to fetch water, he lays a pipe-line to his home. This development is obvious in his behaviour too. Every human society adds its own stock of behaviour which overlies and modifies that which preceded it. This added stock is called culture. The overlay is never identical in two different societies because it is not inborn.

Culture represents all those things which are not inherited biologically. It involves those things which have been accepted as ways of thinking or doing or behaving. When these ways are taught by one person to another they become patterns of behaviour. Let us take a simple example of human culture. A digging stick is a stick of a particular kind for digging up vegetables. Apes will use sticks but they will wave them around at random. For an ape a stick is a toy not a tool. The stick will not be shaped, used, handed on as a regular necessity of chimp life. To men, however, such things are handed on, not merely as objects but as ideas. For men, a digging stick is not just a stick he has around, it is quite definitely a digging stick. It is a stick for digging vegetables. More important, it is not just a stick but a pattern of behaviour. The social group knows about it, uses it and conveys it to others. This known pattern which makes and uses digging sticks is the actual culture item. The same idea may be applied to the use of an animal skin as a robe, or a form of marriage passed on from one society to another.

Culture, therefore, is not just a stock of clever ideas. It is true that man invented culture, but the cultural pattern promptly took charge of man. His culture becomes his whole environment and in fact shapes him. We are creatures of necessity and therefore we possess the culture of our own society. But culture is not the result of any action by an individual, it is the result of the consistent thinking and doing of the social group.

On this reckoning all culture grows out of the past. This does not mean, however, that one society automatically supersedes the one which preceded it. Very often a society will include and amplify the culture items it has received from the past. Yet the transference of truth and the dove-tailing of ideas have been very remarkable. Not every ancient custom becomes a culture item. There is a process of selection and distillation which is going on all the time. It is nothing short of miraculous that in almost every case truth is asserted through the culture items that survive. It seems as if these culture items bore a hall-mark which ensured their approval and acceptance. Although St. Paul was not thinking of the persistence of culture items when he wrote "For we have no power to act against the truth, but only for it" (N.E.B. 2 Cor. 13: 8), man's social and cultural development gives him the warmest support.

One form of culture is practical and utilitarian, while another becomes artistic and spiritual. The man who takes the simple tool with which he has tilled the soil and buries it in the earth as an offering to his god, is really indicating the close connexion between culture and religion.

THE SIGN IDEA AND COMMUNICATION

Signs. There are certain sayings and cliches which have become part of our language and it maybe they will give us a clue to the origins of speech. Consider the following: learning by doing, we want deeds not words, every picture tells a story, oral tradition, the highest cannot be spoken, words fail me, say it with flowers—all of which suggest not only that mime preceded speech but that it is also an effective and telling medium of communication. A little girl will go through the entire ritual of bathing and dressing her doll long before she is able to express in words what she is doing. It is true that this may be due to imitation, but it proves that something has been communicated to her. Perhaps this points to the beginning of communication. Certainly man had to find some way of expressing his thoughts, feelings and desires intelligibly. Before he knew the meaning of words or could speak them, there seems little doubt that he would communicate by means of signs, gestures and curious antics of one sort or another. Some gestures have survived and often take the place of words, such as nodding the head, shrugging the shoulders, and waving farewell.

Animals cannot give a command in words but they can make signals to one another. A monkey signals to her young that she is ready to move on, the baby clings to its mother knowing she is about to leap to another tree. A sambur pricks up its ears and the whole herd is alerted. No doubt facial expression also played a part, and the expression 'if looks could kill' still has meaning.

However, signs and gestures, facial expressions and attitudes, are not much use unless they are understood and interpreted. A man may see a tiger with head, body and tail close to the ground, but he has to learn that it is not having a siesta but is in the last stages of stalking its prey and is ready to pounce. Unless he can interpret this gesture correctly, his life is in danger. On the other hand, he may see a member of his tribe waving a spear in his hand, but he has to learn that such a man is not bubbling over with joy but that he is ready to kill. In other words a gesture by itself accomplishes nothing, it has to be interpreted and its message taken. All these gestures will result in particular reactions and the nature of the reaction will indicate to what extent the gesture has been understood. At least in a crude but effective way communication will have been made.

Sounds. If however the tiger had been snarling and the man with the spear had been making angry noises, the onlookers would have had little doubt about the evil intention. Sound would endorse the evidence of sight and this would be a further step in the process of understanding. They would react to different sounds in different ways. Growls and angry shouts would prompt one reaction, exclamations of pain, another, while laughing and singing would prompt yet another. Even in describing these gestures we have already put names to them, but it is likely that in the earliest times the emotional reaction to the three instances we have given would be such sounds as 'Oh,' 'Ow' and 'Ha ha.'

In fact, an important development was made when it was discovered that certain things made characteristic noises and that these noises could be easily recognized. Of course such noises would have to be learned by memory if they were to be applied to future occasions. They were not yet fixed to definite symbols like words, nevertheless, it was quite an advance.

A further step forward was made when it was realised that such sounds might be imitated. In some cases in our own language the insect or animal has suggested the word; a bee really does buzz, a snake hisses, a duck quacks, and a tiger growls. Men were able then to proceed to the inference: all snakes do this and all ducks do that, and this simplified matters immensely.

Sentences. We have not yet reached the most significant development. We have reached the stage of words but not the stage of a language. A language requires something more than speech, it requires not only symbols, but categories and sentences. Consider the sentence: "I saw a jet plane lying on the motorway." This does not only give a signal, a single gesture, but it presents to the mind the picture of an event. It conveys a plane, a crash, excitement, a traffic hold-up, police, ambulance, and many other things. Questions are asked and a discussion follows. One of the points that arises is that a man is taking notes. He does this because he cannot trust his memory to be absolutely reliable three weeks hence. Later he had to give a report, evidence, facts. He could only do this properly if he committed it to writing on the spot. And here is another clue: before symbols were written everything depended on memory, but this demanded the almost impossible feat of applying exactly the same words to the same events. There was only one way and that was to put these symbols in permanent form so that they could be applied to future occasions. Consequently, when a handful of Greek soldiers scribbled an inscription on an Egyptian temple in B.C. 700 they had originated the art of writing and had given to one method of communication a permanent form.

Yet words had to be found for all sorts of occasions and situations, and this involved forming categories. It is not enough to say, "Cities are places where there are houses," for there are houses in hamlets, villages and towns. It follows that distinctive words must be found for these different categories. Nor does the above definition tell us anything about the kinds of houses. They may be made of snow, wood, stone, brick, mud, coconut palm, and so another category of words was needed to describe the kinds of houses.

Again it had to be known which words were interchangeable and which were not. To say that England had one hot day last summer does not mean that she has a tropical climate. So while the weather was good on that day, the climate is temperate. The weather refers to specific occasions but 'climate' refers to the over-all picture. In a living language words are always changing their meaning, and new words being added. Some words added in recent years are: astronaut, automation, space, nuclear-physics, apartheid, pop, mod, rocker and the rest. Categories arise for which we are not equipped and we have to invent new words to fit the new situation.

Yet words alone are meaningless, they have meaning only when linked with other words. The sentence is really the story of civilization at the cross-roads. Unless a sentence had been spoken and understood, we should have had a language of stunted growth and the progress of civilization would have been virtually impossible. A sentence is a statement of connected ideas. When man had reached the stage of communicating ideas through sentences, he had attained not only culture but also the beginnings of civilization. Culture depends upon language, and society depends upon culture. Religion could have made no impact upon society without a means of communication. This is the vital link in the whole process of the development of society. For language is the crucial bridge which man must cross if he is to pass from ignorance to knowledge, from barbarianism to civilization, from superstition to religion.

THE CASTE IDEA AND SOCIETY

The caste system is usually associated with Hinduism. When the Aryans first entered India from the north in approximately 2000 B.C. they brought with them a very highly-developed social and economic system, and the first thing to be said about it is that it was based on their Vedas (Scriptures). In them Purusha is described as the primeval man from whom the four castes orginated:

> His head became the Brahmin,
> And from his arms was the Rajanya made,
> His thighs became the Vaisya,
> And from his feet the Sudra was produced.

This gives for all time the order of precedence in the four castes: Brahmin, Rajanya or Kshatriya, Vaisya and Sudra. It was regarded as essential for the smooth and efficient working of an ordered society that it should be divided into four distinct groups. This division was based on calling or vocation: the Brahmin was to fulfil the sacred law and care for the souls of the people; the Rajanya was to protect the people against their enemies; the Vaisya was to attend to the cattle and cultivate the land, while the Sudra was to be the meek servant of the other castes. All this seems very good—priest, soldier, farmer and labourer are all necessary for the proper functioning of society, but like many other good things, it went wrong. It went wrong because the religious sanction ousted every other consideration. The religious origin of caste has made its laws invariable and in many ways this has been the curse of India. It has led to rivalries, conflicts, family feuds and many other difficulties.

But all these things have been mild in their effects when compared with the terrible consequences of the system in relation to those outside it. The effects of the caste system, its exclusiveness and uncharitableness, have been felt most keenly by the Dravidians who have had no means of redress and yet no escape from it. The only sin that the Dravidians have committed is that they happen to be outside the caste system. It is true that attempts are being made to rectify this system with its attendant evils, but things move slowly in India and nothing more slowly than reform. Even Gandhi's attempt to win temple entry for the outcastes has not had the desired effect.

It is possible to have a neatly worked-out social and economic system which is doomed to failure because of inherent weaknesses in it. Despite its early promise it has been almost universally rejected as a possible system of society for other countries. But this might be excused if the system had succeeded in India itself. Its only success has been the complete isolation of caste Hindus from their brethren in India. Yet this has brought misery, poverty and illiteracy in its train. It is for these reasons that the caste system must be dismissed as a possible system of human society. A happy and efficient society does not lie that way.

THE COVENANT IDEA AND RELIGION

Perhaps no concept has made such a profound impression upon society as that of a Covenant initiated by God. We must now consider its origin, its nature, its terms and its scope.

The origin of the Covenant. Sometimes an agreement is made between persons of equal standing. Abraham and Abimilech had a difference and eventually came to an agreement. In such a case two parties voluntarily and of their own free-will come to a mutual agreement. But the Covenant which God makes with people is different. Here it is an arrangement between two *unequal* partners. The one responsible for the Covenant is God alone. God initiates it and He alone lays down its terms. Addressing Moses God said: "I am Yahweh," and ever afterwards the people said: "Our God is called Yahweh and we are the people of Yahweh." Imparting a name means imparting a nature and involves a lasting relationship. Now a relationship cannot exist without assuming a clear form, and the form is a Covenant. When God reveals Himself He uses the ideas and concepts of men, and they certainly understood something about agreements. But it should be remembered that the idea that the Hebrews should be the People of God was not a convenient human arrangement, nor was it an invention of men, it was God's will. The Covenant made a nomadic society God's possession. This new relationship is not to be thought of as simply an idealistic calling but as an experience through which the people must pass. They are now in an immediate relationship with God as His pledged servants. It will be clear that such an idea marks an entirely new development in divine-human relationships.

The nature of the Covenant. If the keeping of the Covenant on the divine side is certain, why should there be a Covenant at all? It was necessary for Israel's sake. The spiritual relationship had to be established by a concrete, contractual agreement. "And I have also established my Covenant with them" (Ex. 6: 4). The use of the word 'establish' means that it is now a fact as distinct from a promise as it had been previously. And this was all the more necessary if their unity as a nation was to be guaranteed. They now belonged to Yahweh by election, consecration and mission, and the Covenant was the irrevocable seal of this threefold privilege. Their fellowship with God had passed from the potential to the factual. In establishing His Covenant with them He revealed His Covenant-love, and this was an indication not only of His character but also of His attitude to His people.

The terms of the Covenant. There is no Covenant without conditions and in this case the conditions were the ten commandments given at Sinai. These are so familiar to us now that we are apt to forget that any one of them taken alone was capable of bringing about a revolution in human society. Of course the immense significance of these moral and ethical precepts was not realised all at once. Later on, however, the constitution of Israel was regarded as a moral constitution and the ten commandments were undoubtedly the basis of it. To disobey the words given at Sinai meant the forfeiture of their Covenant relationship. Nor is this all, the Covenant was made with the people as a whole and not with individuals. It is true that the individual stands within the Covenant, but the corporate relationship is always emphasized. It is axiomatic of Hebrew thought that the individual can live before God only as a member of society.

The scope of the Covenant. The Hebrews held this idea in trust for all mankind. A solemn mission was committed to them: they were to bring all the peoples of the world to an awareness of a spiritual destiny. The Covenant was to be the divine instrument to hold them true to this mission. Three obligations were laid upon them: to obey the Commandments, to keep the Covenant, and to fulfil their mission. Only so would they become what they were intended to be "a light for all people" (Isa. 42: 6). But if they succeeded in this, the Psalmist's prayer would be answered, "And all the ends of the earth shall fear Him." (Ps. 67: 7) Sufficient has been said to show that nowhere is the social function of religion more forcibly expressed than in the Covenant idea.

CHAPTER IX

MONOTHEISM

THE PROBLEM STATED

When we try to understand the being of God we are like the little boy that Augustine found trying to pour all the waters of the sea into a hole which he himself had dug in the sand. But somehow the search must continue for there is something in man which insists on reaching out to the great discovery.

Let us put three questions to an imaginary Brahmin priest. Do you love and honour your gods? The answer is likely to be: "Can a man love a tiger? Can a man honour a triangle?" That is tantamount to saying that he thinks of his gods as angry and vindictive, and the reference to the triangle means that he is thinking in terms of 'things' or impersonal forces rather than persons. His gods are to be feared and he will go to them only when he is in dire trouble. He will go to his gods only as a last resort, but if possible he will steer clear of them.

We may now put a further question: Do you experience in your life a conflict between good and evil? "Evil" he answers, "what is evil?" We explain that evil is to disobey God's will or to flout God's law. He then says: "But who knows God's will? God is above all law. We are happy when God or the gods leave us alone."

The third question is: What do you hope for from this life and the next? The answer is: "Nothing." He explains that all things happen according to our Karma or fate. Then he adds: "But it is night and the new moon, and I am old and don't like to think of death." There is no doubt that these answers would be sincerely given but the question is: do they provide adequate answers to such questions as the nature of God, the problem of evil and the hope of immortality?

It may be argued that Hinduism represents a Polytheistic system and that the same questions put to a Muslim might produce answers that are more adequate. To the first question he would answer: "Allah is great and asks only for submission." To the second he would answer: "I fulfil my religious obligations and leave the rest to Allah," and to the third he would say: "I hope to do the will of Allah and he will not burden my soul beyond its power." It is possible, therefore, to belong to a monotheistic faith and still to know little of the character and purpose of God. Does Hebrew monotheism help us at this point? But first let us define what is meant by Monism and Theism.

DEFINITION OF TERMS

Monism. This doctrine affirms the oneness of all true being. One thing really exists—Brahman, and there is no second. Like salt in water Brahman pervades the whole universe. The Atman—the principle of life in man—is the same as Brahman. To know that these are one is liberation. The world is a cosmic illusion and only exists in the thinking of the ignorant. Man seeks deliverance from the curse of a separate existence and from imprisonment in the world of illusion.

To be caught in ignorance about the eternal unity is error, and this is the cause of unblessedness. The Upanishads make it clear that man is not intended to stay in this state of unblessedness:

> He whose body is the soul and who leads the soul,
> He Himself is thy soul, He the immortal one.

Redemption is possible by the knowledge that Atman is Brahman, and it is then that ignorance is broken and distinctions disappear.

Theism. Theism is the attempt to understand the being of God by looking at the created world and asking: how did it begin, what will be its end, and who gives it purpose and meaning? We begin with things as they are and try to trace 'the first Good, first Perfect, and first Fair.' The argument will be strengthened, however, if we begin with creative will in ourselves and ask whether we are able to do anything without using our will. If we conclude that our will is essential and that our actions are determined by it, it would seem reasonable to suppose that the universe lives and moves by the activity of a supreme creative Will and this may lead us to thoughts about the being of God.

This time we begin with an idea in the mind. Every boy dreams of a perfect girl. But he does not leave it there, he is confident that one day he will meet her. He has no doubt about her existence, he is only waiting to know her. In man's mind there is the idea of a Perfect Being. It may be admitted that the argument is not foolproof, but it does suggest two important lines of thought. It suggests that thought and reality correspond.

> How exquisitely the individual mind to the external world is fitted,
> And how exquisitely too the external world is fitted to the mind.

It also suggests that there are in the world ultimate values and this leads us to assume that somewhere these values are completely realized and embodied. Of course, if it is argued that there are *no* values in the universe, then we must ask whether it makes sense at all. But the latter opinion is not commonly held. In general it is assumed that the world is amenable to reason, akin to the human mind, and responsive to accurate observation and experiment. All this means that it is a dependable world, possessing its own values, and that on the whole these commend themselves to our own sense of right and truth. This is the meaning behind the lines:

> And for the everlasting right,
> The silent stars are strong.

Further, there are evidences of order and design in the world and these generally presuppose the presence of a mind. Even the recognition and appreciation of order and design is a considerable gift and perhaps such a gift ought to be regarded as a divine endowment. We look with astonishment and admiration at the man who is able to measure the distance between Earth and other planets, and we think he is remarkable, but he is hardly more remarkable than the One who set the planets in motion and then gave man the ability to measure their distances. Attempts are often made to dislodge these traditional arguments, but they are not to be dismissed lightly. Their greatest weakness, however, is that they begin with the life of man and seek to deduce truth about God. It is not the ideal method but it is one method and that is why the theistic case has been mentioned here.

A word must be added here about the new slant which Professor Tillich has given to this subject. Tillich is concerned to show that God is the ground of all being. While depth is a dimension of space, it is a spiritual symbol as well. It means the opposite of 'shallow' and 'high.' Truth is deep and not shallow; suffering is depth and not height. The real enlightenment came when philosophers first questioned what everyone had taken for granted—being itself. But there is no depth without the way to depth. Truth without the way to truth is dead. We should pause and listen to the voices speaking to our depth and from our depth. 'Depth Psychology' helps us here because it helps us probe below the surface of self-knowledge. The name of this infinite and inexhaustible ground of all being is God. Indeed depth is what the word God means. The depth of suffering is the door, the only door, to the depth of truth. Yet suffering is not the last word, joy is deeper than suffering and joy comes at the end. Tillich quotes the words of Nietzsche: "Woe says: Hence, go! But joys want all eternity, want deep, profound eternity."

Monotheism. We must first notice that there is a difference between Theism and Monotheism. A Theist looks at the world and man, and then tries to understand God, while a Monotheist receives a revelation and tries to understand man and the world in the light of it. In the main, a Theist is concerned with a way of knowing; a Monotheist is concerned with a way of believing. The first makes his investigations at the philosophic level, the second at the religious level. The Theist asks: What is the Good? How can I know the Good? The Monotheist asks: Who gave the revelation? Is it possible to respond to it and how? Both are looking at the same problem but are seeking to understand it in different ways. The difference is that one looks from the angle of philosophy and the other from the angle of religion.

We must further emphasize that it is impossible to trace a neat and tidy logical development in man's search for God. Apart from the fact that men have held simultaneously many different ideas about God, there is also the fact that even today many people do not hold the monotheistic position. Nevertheless, it is widely held and we must now discover how this idea emerged.

PRIMITIVE MONOTHEISM—HOW DID IT ARISE?

Primitive man was greatly preoccupied with unity, for he soon learned that he could not go it alone. Unity as an ideal was almost as important as the more practical instinct of self-preservation. He sought unity with the totem animal, unity with the spirits of his ancestors, unity within his own tribe, unity with supernatural powers, and indeed he used all his faculties to make unity a reality for his tribe as well as for himself. We have also seen that customs turned into social laws of the tribe and such laws helped to bring about the desired unity.

But he was greatly interested in authority too. There is no doubt that the word 'chief' came very early. The chief of the tribe received the respect of the rest; the chief animal became his totem; among his gods there was a High God who was superior to all the rest, and many of his sacrifices proved that he recognized his dependence on higher powers. It is interesting to note that for the Maoris Io ruled the heavens, and the name Stua which was applied to lower spirits was never applied to him. Io is wise, invisible and without origin. And although they sometimes rebel against the irksomeness of human authority, this they do not question. But in fact the savagery of primitive man is often exaggerated. For the most part primitive man was, and was content to be, man under authority.

He was also concerned with the problem of control. Magic, shamanism, witchcraft and sorcery were all attempts to control in one way or another forces which he did not understand. Those who possessed this astonishing power of controlling other forces, even supernatural ones, received the greatest respect. If a magician had the power to control the habits of a bear and thereby to know its hideout, he would keep it a secret because the power to control anything was greatly prized. Also he would receive the respect and reverence of his tribe if he could demonstrate this power.

Now it will be clear that such a wholesome respect for ideas of unity, authority and control is only a short step to the surmise that perhaps somewhere or in someone all these powers were embodied. It is a concept not as foreign to man's nature as is sometimes supposed.

THE CASE FOR PRIMITIVE MONOTHEISM

This rests on the following points. It is not unreasonable to suppose that together with his desire for truth and his inherent religious endowment, man was given a measure of revelation, sufficient to move him to worship and to seek fellowship with God. And as there is in human thought a powerful impulse to objectify and personify the mysterious and the supernatural, it is possible that this may lead to a genuine monotheism.

But it must be added that Monotheism once accepted, is not necessarily invariable. A degeneration from Monotheism to something less is not unknown in religious history. For instance, a lofty Monotheism was accepted by the Hebrews in Mosaic times but it is not supposed that they never fell away from that high standard. Recent excavations have unearthed a great temple at Mizpah which was consecrated to Ishtar, the Mesopotamian Deity. We also know that in Canaan Hebrew worship was mixed up with the worship of the Phoenician Baal and the Moabite god, Chemosh. Hebrew worship in Canaan was far removed from the early Monotheism of Moses.

An even stronger argument may be deduced from the early religions of India and Egypt. The ancient Hindus believed in the mighty Varuna —the Lord of the High Heavens (1500 B.C.). What they thought of him is revealed in the Vedic hymns:

> Only the Existent One breathed calmly, self-contained,
> Nought else but He there was—nought else above, beyond.
> (Mandala 10, hymn 129)

Or consider this in hymn 121:

> Him let us praise, the golden child
> That rose in the beginning, that was born the Lord,
> The mighty Varuna who rules above,
> Looks down upon these worlds, His kingdom,
> As if close at hand.

Yet all of us know that Hinduism later fell into a Polytheistic system with a pantheon of thousands of gods and goddesses.

Alongside this and about a hundred years later there appeared in Egypt Amenhetep IV who declared to all the world that the gods the Egyptians worshipped were non-existent and that the only Deity was the one who revealed himself through Aten—the Sun Disc. Here we have Monotheism of a very high order, for Amenhetep worshipped not the sun disc itself but the power behind it. He sent out a decree that this was to be the accepted worship of the country. He also changed his name to Akhenaten and built his new capital—Akhetaten which, incidentally is now the village of Tel-el-amarna. Even though this belief was only a phase, it is a very important phase in Egyptian history.

THE CASE AGAINST PRIMITIVE MONOTHEISM

It is argued that the idea of a supreme being or power is not essential to religion. Sometimes even when the idea of a supreme God is accepted, He plays a minor role. Buddhism, for instance, is a religious philosophy which makes no reference to a supernatural power. But just because Buddhism does not make any reference to a supernatural power, it cannot fairly be regarded as a religion.

In primitive religions it is hard to avoid a dualism—an unceasing conflict between powers of Good and powers of Evil. Even in a sublime system like Persian Zoroastrianism the conflict is never resolved. Where Good and Evil compete on an equal footing there is obviously no room for Monotheism.

Where a High God was worshipped, this took place alongside the belief in lesser gods (Henotheism). But where other gods are even recognized, Monotheism cannot be said to exist.

The following conclusions may be drawn from this discussion:

(a) Even before the time of Moses there were hints at Monotheistic belief but there is insufficient evidence to show that it was a widely accepted principle of religious faith.

(b) Where it existed there seems no indication of the character of Supreme Being and this means that Primitive Monotheism remained non-moral and non-ethical.

(c) The Supreme Power was regarded as an object of worship but there is no suggestion of personal relationship between the worshipped and the worshipper. Moreover, no answer is given to the problem of evil which, after all, is one of the main concerns of religion.

HEBREW MONOTHEISM

Monotheism proper must seek to answer such questions as these: Is God the sole Creator? Does God reveal Himself? Is it possible to know the character of God? What does God require of man? Is there hope of redemption?

Yahweh is the living God. He creates life because He is the source of life. He is the cause of all things that come into existence. He creates all things out of nothing. Being the Creator of all things He claims to be the possessor of all things. He is the ruler of the world, and this means that He is not dependent upon anyone else. When we say that God lives, thinks, speaks, decides, we are ascribing to Him personal qualities. God creates, controls and communicates and these are the distinguishing features of His character. This means that man is His creature and that all things come under His rule and serve His purpose.

Yahweh is God alone. "Thou shalt have no other gods apart from Me." He has no pantheon, no assistant, no consort, and He brooks no rivals. Although the Hebrews sometimes worshipped other gods, this was never condoned or excused. They denied that other gods could do what their devotees claimed for them. When other races pointed to their images, the Hebrews denied the force behind the image. In any case, representations of Yahweh were strictly forbidden.

He was different from others in His nature. Just because He was righteous He made moral and ethical demands upon His worshippers. His demands could not be gainsaid because these were linked up with His purpose in history. He was not identified with any natural force but He ruled all of them. He was no storm-god yet He controlled the elements. He was in no sense a fertility god yet nothing possessed life without Him. He made all things serve His purpose of salvation, salvation not only for Israel but for the whole world.

He delivered His people from bondage, He led them like a shepherd, He made a Covenant with them, He controlled their history as well as that of other nations, He promised them a great Deliverer through whom He would be revealed as universal love. This brief outline shows how far the thought of the Hebrews towered over all their rivals. Of course, the day was to come when "the Word became flesh" but that is another story.

PART II

CHAPTER X

THE HEBREWS AND THEIR RELIGION

THE HISTORY OF THE HEBREWS

Everything appeared to be going well for the Hebrews in Egypt until there arose a king "who knew not Joseph." He obviously did not know how much Joseph had done by his careful planning to save the nation in time of famine. Yet the memory of Joseph's statesmanship had remained fresh in the minds of Egyptians for over five hundred years and perhaps it is not surprising that after that length of time the memory began to pale. The king who knew not Joseph was Ramases II (1300–1234). Prior to his reign the Hebrews had been getting along well and had been generously treated. They had been permitted to rear their sheep and pursue their social and religious customs without any interference from the Egyptian government. But the size of the Hebrew community was steadily growing and Ramases, already involved in a conflict with the Hittites, considered that if the tribes of Asiatic origin united against him, the Hebrews would join them. So without giving any reasons and quite unexpectedly he moved the Hebrews from the north-eastern frontier of his kingdom where they were engaged in their harmless, pastoral occupation and subjected them to a system of forced labour. They were constantly reminded of their servile condition by the taskmaster's eye and the lash of his whip. This intolerable situation continued throughout the reign of Ramases. It soon became apparent that his son Merenptah (1234–14) intended to perpetuate the same oppressive system. Just when there seemed no hope of relief from their bondage and suffering, Moses appeared, a young man "instructed in all the wisdom of Egypt." Moses bestrode the scene like a giant. His background, his strength of character, his gifts of leadership, and his sense of mission, combine to make him the type of man most needed by the Hebrews. Pharaoh could not match the moral and spiritual stature of the new leader of the slaves. It is possible that Ramases would have been able to withstand the persistent demands of Moses but Merenptah was weak and vacillating and could not make up his mind whether to keep the Hebrews in his power or let them go. At last he decided that he was struggling against supernatural powers, and as the plagues became more and devastating, his obstinacy broke down and he agreed to let the

71

Hebrews go. Freed from their bondage the slaves lost no time in hurrying towards the frontier, but when they reached Migdol they realized that Pharaoh, who had once again changed his mind, was following them. Pressed by Egyptian horsemen from behind and with only the Red Sea in front of them, it was clear that only a miracle could save them. A strong wind blew with such force during the night that it left the shallow waters low enough to be forded on foot. The wind changed and the Egyptians were unable to cross. The Hebrews attributed this deliverance to Jehovah and the event became for them both the sign and the pledge of divine protection.

Even today the journey across the Sinai desert is a formidable experience, yet they were able to face it with the assurance of divine guidance and all through their journeyings they received many signs of the divine Presence. Moses went up a mountain to pray and when he descended he was sure that he was speaking to the chosen race. It was there that Hebrew religion really began. It is true that the patriarchs had paved the way but the main characteristics of Hebrew religion were first made known on Mount Sinai. The revelation of the true God, the Covenant, the Commandments, and the promise of Canaan, all arise out of the event at Sinai. Whatever happened in later Hebrew history was interpreted in the light of that event.

The journey in the wilderness is important because almost every incident taught them a little more about the character and the requirements of Jehovah. During the absence of Moses in the mountain they had made an image of a golden calf, and after what Moses had seen and heard, this was regarded as an act of sacrilege. At Rephidim they dared to put God to the test and were immediately rebuked. At Kadesh, Korah rebelled against the chosen leaders, and at the same place Moses became faithless and impatient, and for this reason forfeited the privilege of leading his people into Canaan. All these incidents taught them more about the God who was revealing Himself to them. He would not countenance idolatry, disobedience, distrust and rebellion. Forty years may seem a long time for a nation's discipline and training but at least the experience taught the Hebrews lessons they were never to forget. Some of these lessons were:

(a) That it is the holiness of God which distinguishes Him from the gods of other tribes and that this holiness entitles him to reverence and worship.

(b) That God is intimately related to the *everyday life* of His people, their food and drink, trials and triumphs, work and play. No truth stands out more clearly than this in the wilderness wanderings.

(c) That God calls and guides nations as well as individuals. If he raises up a leader and equips him for his task, he also chooses a nation and guides it to its true destiny.

(d) That God brings redemption to His people. He redeems them from slavery to freedom, from the land of Wandering to the land of Promise, from Babylon to the Holy City, and from the power of evil to the life of holiness.

Eventually the land of Promise was reached but the problems in Canaan were scarcely less formidable than the problems they confronted in the desert. There was the question of the integration of the nation, their relationship with other tribes, their attitude to other gods, the rules of worship and the meaning of the cultus, the relation of religion to conduct, the method of government, and the building of a Temple fit for the honour of Jehovah.

They demanded a king and Saul was appointed, followed by David and Solomon. Sadly, due to tribal feuds, the kingdom divided, Ephraim in the North and Judah in the South. The king did not, after all, guarantee the unity of the nation. There followed endless quarrels between North and South, and skirmishes with surrounding tribes. In all these changes and developments one great fact stands out clearly: the key figure in the nation was not the king but the man of God: Samuel, Elijah, Elisha, and other great prophets of both kingdoms. In all matters the opinion of the man of God was sought, and it may safely be said that in Hebrew history the kings were the servants of the prophets.

While Israel and Judah were strong enough to hold their own with petty states like Edom and Moab, the situation was different when they were confronted with the mighty empires of Assyria and Babylon. The Northern Kingdom fell to Assyria in 721 B.C. and the Southern Kingdom to Babylon in 586 B.C. When the Persian Empire was subdued by Alexander (332) Palestine came under the rule of the Greeks. In fact, only for a hundred years (167–63 B.C.) did the Jews experience real independence, and this was due to the revolt of the Maccabees against Antiochus IV Epiphanes, one of the Seleucid kings. All hope of permanent independence was banished because another great empire was on the march, and Jerusalem and its Temple were destroyed by the Romans in A.D. 70. Yet there was one thing which no conqueror could take from the Hebrews, it was Hope.

THE HOPE OF THE HEBREWS

Hebrew history is divided into periods according to the prominence of messianic figures. It is assumed, of course, that Yahweh is present and active in every period of history and this fact determines the people's belief in all messianic figures. In the period before the monarchy the prominent figure was the corporate figure of the people: "I will establish my covenant to be a god unto thee and to thy seed after thee',

(Gen. 17: 7). Naturally during the monarchy the prominent figure was the Davidic King but the Messiah was always thought to be the representative of God as well as of the people. After the destruction of the monarchy future hopes are again centred in the people. The thought here is of God incarnated in the nation of Israel. This view is particularly stressed by the Second Isaiah although even he sometimes appears to think of Cyrus as a possible Messiah. At the Restoration the union of the priestly and kingly idea becomes prominent, and this is because there is a deeper sense of sin, and a Messiah is needed who combines both priestly and kingly functions.

The following points about the people, the prophet and the message ought especially to be noted:

(a) The prominent agent in every age is idealized. This applies when the nation becomes the agent of divine action. Sometimes the reference is to a faithful remnant and sometimes to the nation as a whole. In Daniel, for instance, "the saints of the Most High," who receive the kingdom are the people, and the term 'son of man' is a symbol of the people. Whether the agent of divine action is the whole nation or a remnant or an individual, the emphasis continues to be on the presence and continuous action of God in their midst. The Messiah or Messianic figure in any form is simply the instrument used by God.

(b) The prophet has no place in the eschatological hope of the Hebrews because the function of the prophet is superseded in the perfect state. Hence Jeremiah's word, "I will write my name in their hearts" (Jer. 31).

(c) Moreover the Messianic figure, whatever form he may assume, is commissioned for one purpose—to bring salvation, although it must be remembered that in the Old Testament salvation signifies fellowship with God.

The above outline will make it clear that the Messiah stands for the coming of God in mercy, power and blessing to His people. Since God is the source of all blessing, the purpose of Israel's mission is usually described as making way for the coming of God. This is not merely a coming in wonders, in the words of the prophets, and in terms of spiritual influence, it is objective and personal, "Behold the Lord cometh in might" (Isa. 40). He comes in fullness and usually the age behind him has been wound up and a new age commences. His coming involves the restitution of all things. Not Israel only, but the inanimate world longs for it, "The Lord is king, let the earth rejoice" (Ps. 97: 1). In former ages God had slept but now He awoke and had taken the reins of power. The kingdom was the Lord's. In short, God was fully present in the Messianic King for the purposes of redemption. This is the loftiest messianic concept—the Messiah becomes the personal appearance of God.

THE CALL OF THE PROPHET

Taken. All revelation begins with God. God brings to birth a truth which man needs to know. That truth then becomes objective and enters upon a life of its own. Just because God had taken charge of him, the prophet had the authority of God. When Moses pleaded inadequacy, God said, "See I have made thee a god to Pharaoh and Aaron shall be thy prophet." In Hebrew thinking the initiative is always with God. Amos was 'taken,' and disowned any professionalism. The same compulsion is felt when the prophet says: "The hand of the Lord is upon me." Even though Isaiah seems to contradict this (here am I, send me), it should be remembered that in his case the divine initiative is present in the vision which prompted the prophet's response. Moreover, the prophet has to wait for an answer to his questions. He dare not act without divine prompting.

Broken. When a prophet is entrusted with a divine commission, his task is by no means easy. It often brings him conflict and suffering. He has to say "Thus saith the Lord" whatever the cost to himself. In the Song of the Vineyard (Isa. 5) the Lyric, with which it begins, passes into the first person in the third verse: "Judge, I pray you, between me and my vineyard." The real secret of the prophet's power was his identification with God. Amos, tortured by the injustice and oppression which he saw all around him; Jeremiah commanded to proclaim the destruction of the Holy City; and Hosea broken in spirit again and again as he seeks to win back his partner from the ways of unfaithfulness; all these show that before a man can be a true instrument of God he must be broken and that this is the sole precondition of true identification. First he is taken, then broken, then given.

Given. It is this fact which explains the virtual identification of the prophets with God. God had given them a message but He had also given them. Often they used the formula, "Thus saith the Lord" but sometimes they spoke on the Lord's behalf without even using that formula. The fact that he is 'given' frees the prophet from the expediencies and compromises of the ordinary politician and keeps alive in him the sense of mission. But having been called of God and having been prepared for his task by conflict and suffering, he is ready to be given in the service of the world.

THE MESSAGE OF THE HEBREWS

It concerned the past. Here prophecy found its chief material and its most significant content. It is in the arena of history that they struggle to vindicate God, not unconsciously like Job, but in the awareness of a divine commission. The prophet showed that changing political circumstances could be transformed into firmly-controlled activities of

God. Yet history for the prophet was always salvation history. There was the call to remembrance, and this was always the appeal to history. Indeed their history was the story of God's dealings with them. They were to remember the rock from which they were hewn. They were to remember the One who had led them and fed them and blessed them. But above all they were to remember the God who had delivered them. They had been slaves in Egypt and at the mercy of Pharaoh; they had been exposed to famine and drought in the wilderness; they had been surrounded by enemy tribes in Canaan; they had been tempted to bow the knee to Chemosh and Baal; after their defeat they had been in subjection to the Babylonians, the Assyrians and the Persians, and many nations greater than theirs had been lost in oblivion. In that long story of defeat and trial and conflict, who had delivered and sustained and led them? It was the living God. Without His aid they could not have survived, and their history is summed up in the words, "Our God is able to deliver us." So they were called upon to remember the past and this gave them not only a sense of thanksgiving but courage for the present.

It concerned the present. The prophets were not only historians, they had a trenchant and relevant message for the present. They always referred to the past in order to point to their message for the present. The past warns: "Go to Shiloh and see what I did to it for the wickedness of my people" (Jer. 7: 12). But the past also encourages for they had an inexhaustible God who was always prepared to do something more. Isaiah 43 tells of many remarkable things that God had done for His people, yet in the middle of it we read: "I will do a new thing." The prophets were mainly concerned with contemporary affairs and for them God was the Great Contemporary. Their message revealed that God was at the centre of the present situation and this introduced into Hebrew prophecy a unifying principle that is not easily traced in the history of other nations. The pattern of unity was evidence of the hidden purpose of God and this meant that past, present and future were telescoped into a coherent whole.

One of the reasons why the eighth century prophets (Amos, Hosea, Micah and the First Isaiah) were so concerned with social evils—injustice, oppression and exploitation—was because in their thinking the goal of the kingdom of God was to be realized on earth. They were forthright and denunciatory because in truth they saw little sign of the kingdom for which they were looking. This fact gave a cutting edge to their words, and all their bright dreams of the future did not blind them to the stern moral demands of the present. Nevertheless there was a future for Israel and the shape of things to come was to be determined by their response in the present.

It concerned the future. One of the interesting facts about human experience is that against all reason there is a spirit of resilience and optimism. All nations hope for a bright tomorrow, and present darkness only serves to accentuate the hope. What did the prophets say about the Day of the Lord? Although the phrase refers to *the* Day, it is not meant to signify *a* Day, but it refers rather to a time or an epoch than a day.

It is a time of light. It brings to a focus the manifestation of the divine purpose in history. It throws light on the nature of revelation, for it is a time when God acts rather than speaks. It means that God will intervene in the course of history, inaugurate a new kingdom ruled over by the Messiah, and gather in all the scattered members of the Jews and the Gentiles also.

It is a time of darkness. This is not altogether a contradiction. It maybe that the time of light will be preceded by a time of darkness and judgment. Malachi asks: "Who shall abide the time of His coming?" Obadiah addresses his people: "Thy reward be upon thine own head." The immediate consequences of the coming of that time could not be viewed with equanimity. Amos says it will be a time of darkness, not light, and Joel declares that even the morn shall be dark. The main point is that it will be a time of judgment. This judgment concerns nations rather than individuals, and it will apply to Israel as well as to the Gentiles. Sometimes it will be brought about through the abnormal phenomena of nature, but normally it will take place through the normal agencies of nature. According to Amos the time was imminent,

> *Fallen, no more to rise,*
> *is the virgin Israel;*
> *forsaken on her land,*
> *with none to raise her up*

for he utters his dirge over Israel (5: 1–2) as if she had already fallen.

It is a time of transformation and triumph. It will mean the absolute transformation of the earth. The mountain of the Lord will be exalted and a new heaven and earth will be created. As far as Israel is concerned this will mean that she is seen to be the People of God and fully restored to her true relationship to God. For the whole world it means that God is shown to be victorious in the present world order and that a new era will be ushered in where justice, peace and prosperity will be revealed.

THE WISDOM OF THE HEBREWS

The greatest example of Hebrew wisdom is the Book of Job (400 B.C.). The poignancy of Job's problem could only be felt by a man who believed in God. The man who says that God's character cannot be known will not be troubled when God acts out of character. The fatalist who believes that everything inevitably follows its appointed course will not trouble to ask the questions which Job asked. Again, a man who rules out spiritual values altogether will not undergo a sense of guilt whatever may befall him. So it is important to emphasize that Job's problem was accentuated because he believed in God.

His problem was: how can the suffering of the righteous be harmonised with the righteousness of God? He accepted that God was the sole Creator and Sustainer of the universe and he also acknowledged God's care over His people as a nation. He was aware that sometimes a nation must pass through difficult and perilous times, but it was not the nation's agony that troubled him, it was his own. He saw the whole problem in sharper focus when the calamities struck at him. The general issue he could forget, the personal one he could not.

He was distracted by God's persecution of him in the present because he could not forget God's kindness in the past. This appeared to mean that God had changed His attitude. The Greeks, for instance, would have had no difficulty here for their gods changed their attitudes as well as their characters with amazing regularity. But Job, believing in an unchanging, righteous God, was faced with a real difficulty. Was this God who now appeared to be hostile and vindictive, the God he had known in the past?

Those who came ostensibly to reassure him only deepened his perplexity. One of them stressed the overwhelming majesty of God. God was great and man but dust and ashes, who then could hope to oppose God? Another emphasized the righteousness of God. How then could man who is unrighteous challenge the actions of God who is righteous? Yet another asserted that the unsearchable wisdom of God should never be questioned by man. Forceful as were these arguments, they did not satisfy Job. He listened to the argument about power and answered: "Will he contend with me in the greatness of his power? nay, but He will give heed unto me." He knew that God's greatness was to make men strong and not to condemn them. Further, just because God was righteous He would vindicate Job in the end: "I know that my Vindicator lives, and that he will stand up at the last upon the earth." Job knew that God was wise and had no need to be told, and it is on this ground that Job declares: "He knows the way that I take." The wise God had taught Job wisdom too: "The fear of the Lord, that is wisdom, and to depart from evil is understanding."

Such questions were answerable, but there was a more searching one. His friends approached him with the calm assumption that sin alone accounted for misfortune. Job's reasoning at this point presents a clear step forward in man's religious development. Job was by no means persuaded that the orthodox view of his time that suffering follows sin, was correct. But he was more puzzled by the suffering which seemed to be inflicted on the righteous. He reasserts his faithfulness to God, and declares that nothing will shake his faith and that he will hold on to the good life whatever arguments his friends may use. "Till I die I will not put my integrity from me. My righteousness I hold fast and will not let it go." He acknowledged the power of God over all life, confessed his inability to solve the problem, and said that he was prepared to wait to find out what God was doing.

He was sustained by three great truths: first, the fact that God is unchanging in his righteousness. He could not forget God's friendliness in the past and the memory of it sustained him. Second, he did not believe that God's present hostility represented his permanent character. It was but a passing phase. But he was puzzled by the thought that the old happy fellowship might be restored when it was too late. Third, and contrary to the thought of his day, he believed that ultimately he would be permitted to see God and in that moment the vision would also bring the answers.

Job finds new hope in the answers that God gives. He receives the divine approval. He had been right in viewing everything in the light of God's purpose. But he must learn some new lessons. He must not separate the God of the world of nature from the God who is related to human life:

> The voice that rolls the stars along
> Speaks all the promises.

Moreover, in order to understand God's ways, it was necessary to know God. Therefore Job must endeavour to centre his thoughts on God and not on himself. He must not lay down the terms on which God must meet him for that would be no more than human presumption. He must also learn that sometimes God's answer is to leave man with a question, and indeed sometimes with a whole series of questions. In chapters 38 and 39 Job is almost overwhelmed with an avalanche of questions from God. "Where wast thou when I laid the foundations of the earth? Who has put wisdom in the inward parts or given understanding to the mind? Who provides for the raven his food?" Job should ponder these things and then ask himself whether it is conceivable that one man should have been excluded from these blessings.

In fact, the point of the drama would be lost if neat and clear-cut answers were given. It would also be untrue to life where sometimes the answer is not known. Job had to be left in ignorance so that he might trust God even if he did not know the reasons for God's actions. He listens to the words: "Acquaint now thyself with Him and be at peace." This is the secret—in the knowledge of God he will find peace. So the story ends with Job reaching a state of mind where, although the problem remains, it troubles him no longer. He is able to say: "Though he slay me, yet will I trust him." In happier days he had heard about God: "I have heard of thee with the hearing of the ear," yet the storms and calamities had not been without their lessons: "but now mine eye seeth Thee."

That is an example of Hebrew Wisdom: it is the story of the pilgrimage of a soul, and it is given here in some detail so that we should not overlook that part of Hebrew literature which is without parallel in the pre-Christian world.

CHAPTER XI

BABYLON, ASSYRIA AND PERSIA

BABYLON (APPROX. 1750–1350 B.C.)

Hammurabi. Babylon was a very large city when Hammurabi (1750 B.C.), the wisest of ancient rulers, came to the throne. It had a network of canals and a rich hinterland of corn and barley fields, as well as orchards and palm groves. It was indeed the forerunner of that walled, turreted Neo-Babylon of Nebuchadnezzar long after in the sixth century, which was dominated by the eight-storied Tower of Babel. On his own confession, Hammurabi was a ruthless man: "I cut down my enemies like dolls of clay." But we have better reasons than that for remembering him. He had a fine logical mind and, on the whole, he used it for the good of his people, for their moral as well as their material good. If he was proud of his achievements, perhaps he had reason to be. "I dug the canal named Hammurabi which brings copious water to the lands of Sumer and Akkad. The top of the wall of Sippar I raised with earth like a great mountain."

On the shoulders of this great ruler lay the task of ruling a very complex society with over two millenia of civilized life behind it. He provided a well-ordered and highly organized economy. Slave owning was not caste ridden as was the case later in Rome and India. There was no coinage at that time, but Hammurabi moved in that direction when he introduced standardized silver bars and shekels. Business contracts were witnessed and ratified, deeds of partnership drawn up, property was registered, and elaborate wills devised. Produce was ample and there was much wheat for chapatis, as popular in India now as in Babylon then, and plenty of barley for beer. The date harvest brought them not only a staple food, but also treacle and arack wine. Oranges, melons and apricots were plentiful. Merchants from India and Iran brought metals and precious stones, and the flocks and herds provided wool and leather. Cedarwood from Lebanon and the Taurus secured a great price. This is the picture of a thriving and progressive society and the real secret was due to a new factor introduced by Hammurabi himself—the laws.

The Laws. These laws will stand for all time as the greatest single contribution to the life and development of society in that or any other age. Hammurabi's greatness lies in seeing the need for such laws, in formulating them and in making them work. They are based on three great principles:

(a) That all classes, including slaves, must be protected.

(b) That all classes must be provided for.

(c) That all classes must be enabled to make progress in the interests of the state as a whole.

This new factor which was introduced by Hammurabi may be summed up in the phrase 'people matter,' for almost every law reveals a dominating concern for the welfare of people; they also reveal a care and compassion which are rare at any time. Blood revenge was prohibited partly because it was cruel and partly because it was senseless. It should be noted that the Hebrews were still holding on to the 'eye for an eye' doctrine long after Hammurabi's reforms. But there was concern for the family as well as the individual. This is shown in the rules regarding marriage, adoption and bequest. The modernity of these laws is altogether astonishing, and the following so-called modern problems are dealt with: exemption from military service, fixity of land tenure, compensation for agricultural improvements, control of the liquor traffic, legal rights for women and children, and a host of other matters.

These laws, although sometimes severe, are reasonable and are certainly a landmark in civilized government. They bear the stamp of public authority and the idea of empire, and both these factors were cultivated and applied by Persia, Rome, and much later by our own empire also.

Art. From the point of view of art Babylon and Assyria must be taken together because their similarities are far more impressive than their differences. On the whole their art was magnificent but uninspired, it was comprised mainly of heavy winged bulls and muscle-bound lions. Much more significant was their use of glazed tiles which later were used extensively in the mosques of Iran. Their border patterns anticipate the designs of Kashmir carpets, and they excelled in depicting hunting and battle scenes in bas-relief.

But their art was essentially practical and down-to-earth and is not characterized by the abstract and symbolic forms of Egypt and China, for instance. They were essentially men of action and their art reveals it. But what it does not reveal is the precise and clear-cut concepts which we might reasonably have expected from the countrymen of Hammurabi.

They were mighty hunters, bending bows from light chariots, and therefore their artists depicted the rush of the chase, the leap of the great hounds, and their roaring prey. The serried ranks of their spearmen and archers have an impressive, rigid monotony. But as long as pictures of their dark faces and square-cut black beards and curled locks remain, we shall have enough to remind us of the strong and resolute, even if sometimes cruel, warriors of Babylon and Assyria.

Astronomy. The study of art not only stimulated mathematics but also strengthened man's grip on reality. But against this there is the infinite loss expressed by the conviction that the real world was the sky-world, and that contemplation of the stars was the only worthwhile activity. It was assumed also that this was the only way of keeping in contact with reality. We still hear of 'sky pilots' and of 'pie in the sky' and this shows that the world has still not outlived this particular Babylonian myth. The stars possessed tremendous power for the Babylonians who cried:

You brilliant stars, you bright ones,
To destroy evil did Anu create you;
At your command mankind was named,
Give the word, and with you let the great ones stand,
Give my judgment, make my decision.

Although the two worlds are distinct, there is one point of similarity. Just as God inhabited an earthly temple so he also inhabited a heavenly temple which was a replica of the earthly one. On this theory we have another world of reality of which earthly forms are a mere imitation, reflection, and an imperfect copy. But it does mean that duality has become static, for since the earthly city is but a reflection of the heavenly, it cannot improve upon it. The temple archetype was to be seen in the constellations. Chaldean maps show sky regions corresponding to earth regions. The Chinese held a related theory: sorrow and war on earth are the reflection of disturbance in the elements, and where there is quiet in the world of nature, it is reflected on earth in peace and joy.

As far as the Babylonians were concerned this theory resulted in one bad thing: it gave the impression that life on earth was unreal and unimportant. But it resulted in a good thing as well: it gave the analogy of the stars and the temple which is part of St. John's vision.

In curious ways Babylonian astronomy still regulates our lives. The seven-day week with days dedicated to the seven planets (these include, of course, the sun and the moon), was adopted quite suddenly all over western Europe in the first century A.D. and this stems from Babylon. The minute and everything counted in sixties is a strange reminder of the thinkers of Babylon.

From 1350 B.C. until 600 B.C. the Assyrians were in control of the old Babylonian Empire. Nevertheless Babylon revived, though never to her former greatness, in what is known as the Chaldean Period. It was during this period that they had intimate contact with the Jews, but we must first look at the Assyrian Empire.

ASSYRIA 1350–625 B.C.

The characteristics of the people. In the second millennium Babylon grew weak and in the north a new race arose, the children of Asshur (the Assyrians) who conquered Babylon about 1300 B.C. The first thing that

took place was a sort of regional crystallization around the great cities—
Asshur, Nimrod and Nineveh. The second thing was to add to the
number of these cities. As a consequence the Assyrians became not only
determined rulers but also forged an instrument of war unrivalled in
size and quality. They were a warlike and disciplined people whose
leaders had wills of iron. The soldiers were rigorously trained and, on
the whole, the leaders were unscrupulous men who were bent on world
conquest.

In the main, the Babylonians were agriculturalists and traders, and
religion counted for more in their public economy than the arts of war.
The Assyrians were a warrior race and their kings commanded a strong
military nobility. Their history is a story of war and conquest. They
inherited their culture from Babylonia.

The community was divided into three classes. First came the aris-
tocracy composed of King, nobles, the priesthood, government officials
and regular soldiers. The second consisted of merchants, farmers and
artisans, and the third consisted of slaves, some of whom had been
captured in war and others had been enslaved through debt or some
criminal offence. It is likely that these class-distinctions were of military
origin. Whether there is a connection between this system and the caste
system in India it is difficult to say but there are striking similarities.
The main difference is that in India the regular soldiers constituted a
caste of their own.

Assyrian religion. Asshur, from whom the Assyrians took their name,
was the national god, and they always gave lip service to him, but he was
very much a figure-head god and was much more impersonal than the
triads in the pantheon, as we shall now see.

In the first of these triads there was Anu, the high god, who corres-
ponds to the sky god, Zeus, in Greek religion. His abode was the third
heaven, he was sometimes known as 'Father,' his shrine was surmounted
by the divine horned cap, and his sacred number was 60.

The second god in the triad was Enlil, a storm god. Eventually he
took precedence over the other two. Although he was the Creator of
mankind, he was also bitterly hostile to man and was the cause of many
calamities. His main function was to be the guardian of the 'tablets of
destiny.'

The third was Enki (later Ea) who was the god of the lands. In
contrast to Enlil he was kindly disposed towards man. He was the
instructor of mankind and revealed to men the mysteries of writing,
building and agriculture. His son was Marduk and together they did
many wonderful things in response to many incantations.

In the second triad there were Sin the moon god, Shamash the sun
god, and Adad the storm god. Their associated female figure was

Ishtar. The latter assumed a much greater importance than the others and became known as 'the goddess.' While she was the goddess of love and procreation, she was also the goddess of war.

Alongside all this was a strange attachment to the sacred tree. The tree was a symbol of strength rather than fertility and the Assyrians were particularly interested in strength. This may be one reason why the religious side of Assyrian life remained cold and stiff. A basic motif in worship was a bare trunk supported by metal bands. It is not known whether the metal band was to reinforce the strength of the tree or merely to mark it out as sacred.

Yet the main form of worship centred round the Emperor who was himself a sign of strength and victory. He too was sacred. In an atmosphere laden with religion and steeped in sorcery there moved the hieratic and heroic figure of the King. Whenever he showed himself with his face uncovered, his worshippers would prostrate themselves before him. The mighty Emperor presided over his vassals and looked on as his captives were numbered. His courage on the field of battle or in the lion hunt appeared to entitle him to the worship of his people. Seeming omnipresent and always self-sufficient, he was the lord of destiny. Not only were the gods with him, he was one of them. In this and in many other ways he anticipated the Caesars of Rome.

Remarkable Assyrian achievements. The oft-told story of the cruelty, oppression and tyranny of Assyrian conquerors must not blind us to the truly remarkable story of Assyrian achievements. It is sometimes said that their sole advance was to build in stone as well as in brick but this is an unfair and over-simplified judgment.

In the first place, a new metal, iron, was discovered and this was a brand new invention. Since the smelting of iron is very different from the smelting of copper, they were faced with a new problem. It is to their credit that they conquered in this field as in many others. Iron-working was known in Assyria in about 1350 B.C. and the use of it spread rapidly in the following two hundred years.

Secondly, measurements became standardized, especially the idea of payments in trade. Silver was used as a medium of exchange and the temples issued silver bars stamped with their weight and the certification of the temple. This advance eliminated the necessity of weighing out silver for every transaction.

Thirdly, a brilliant advance was made in writing. Twenty-nine Sumerian signs were selected to stand for basic simple sounds alone. It was a true alphabet which could spell anything. This was the beginning, and shortly afterwards (1200 B.C.) somewhere in Phoenicia a completely new set of signs (22) was used for the same purpose and from this alphabet those we know in history are derived: Hebrew, Arabic, Sanscrit and our own.

Further, since war was their main concern it is to be expected that significant advances would be made in this sphere also. They introduced cavalry to supplement their chariots and replaced annual conscription by a standing army.

There remains another outstanding contribution. They established an elaborate hierarchy of officials, a sort of Assyrian Civil Service, and imposed an annual fixed tribute on the provinces they conquered. When all these things are considered it will be seen that it is unjust to dismiss the Assyrians as no more than merciless barbarians. Nevertheless there was an element of barbarism in the attitude of the Assyrian conquerors to their vanquished foes.

The Assyrian conquerors. In relation to other states Assyria had three aims: conquest, colonization and consolidation. Her greatest rulers were those who were most successful in achieving any or all of these. Shalmaneser I (1300–1275) was the first Emperor to have dreams of empire, and he soon took control of Babylon. But he found the task so exacting that he did not take his campaign any further. He was soon to learn the lesson that to rule is more difficult than to fight. He appeared to think that the conquest of Babylon was more important than anything else and was the first to style himself 'King of the World.' It is fair to add that he wanted to be remembered as a builder, and to this end he built a new palace in Kalakh and also restored the sanctuary of Ishtar. Shalmaneser was followed by several rulers who accomplished little and during this time Babylon reasserted her independence. This pattern was to be repeated many times in the undulating story of Assyria and Babylon. Then there arose in 1120 a more resolute conqueror and a more capable administrator than any of his predecessors, Tiglath Pileser I. He conquered the whole of Babylonia and added Syria to his trophies. Nor is this all; he himself tells us: "42 countries have I conquered with my own hand." He also tells us that he was interested in travel and wanted most of all to meet people of other nations. Fortunately he left us a record of his many journeys and campaigns in his annals; unfortunately he tells us much more about Pileser than about the people of other races in whom he claimed an interest. We see the true picture when we remember that he visited no country that he did not conquer. But he carried Assyrian rule as far as the Mediterranean, and a King as far away as Egypt lost no time in sending him costly presents. Clearly there were some diplomats around as well as warriors.

A conqueror is always faced with two important problems: he has to find out how to consolidate his gains and colonize his conquered states, and how to use them to the maximum advantage. In the strategy of war he has to use a conquered state as a base and a jumping-off ground for his next campaign, and by some method of taxation he has to compel his satellites to finance his future campaigns. In this twofold task many of the Assyrian rulers were not very successful. They had no thought-out system of holding down the territories they had won. Ultimately, failure in these two respects cost them their empire. In the ninth century they relied only on cruelty. So far we have not emphasized this undesirable trait in the Assyrian character and even now we shall allow one sentence to tell the dismal story. It concerns the methods of Ashur-nasir-pal (883–859): "His usual procedure after the capture of a hostile army was to burn it, and then to mutilate all the grown male prisoners by cutting off their hands and ears and putting out their eyes; after which they were piled in a great heap to perish from sun, flies, their wounds and suffocation; the children, both boys and girls, were burnt alive at the stake, and the chief was carried away to Assyria to be flayed alive for the king's delectation." Of course we allow that there is cruelty in all war, but this is something different, it is the nadir of cruelty. Who will defend cruelty as a principle? Nevertheless it seems to have been accepted as such by some of the Assyrian conquerors. We may recall the words of the prophet Nahum when he heard of the fall of Assyria: "There is no assuaging your hurt, your wound is grievous. All who hear the news of you clap their hands over you. For upon whom has not come your unceasing evil?" (Nahum 3: 19).

There is evidence to believe that even the Assyrians were looking for a system less cruel but equally effective of treating their vanquished foes. Tiglath Pileser III (745–727) instituted the idea of holding down conquered territories by deporting the cream of the population and, as is well known, this is what happened to the citizens of Damascus and later to those of Jerusalem. This method is tinged with its own brand of cruelty but it clearly shows a more humanitarian regime. Assyria was now at the zenith of her power and Sargon I conquered Egypt. After him Sennacherib was left to deal with revolts in Egypt, Elam, Babylon and Syria. A long struggle ensued with the first two of these but by 650 Assyria had become utterly exhausted and had neither the strength nor the will to carry on the struggle. An alliance between the Medes and the Scythians ended Assyria's inglorious rule.

The story of the resurgence of Babylon or Chaldea may be briefly told. It lasted from 625–550. The Medes joined with the Babylonians and divided the Syrian empire. Necho of Egypt (609) was not going to give in easily and marched to challenge Nebuchadnezzar who was now the all-powerful king of Babylon. On the way Necho defeated King Josiah at Megiddo but was himself defeated by Nebuchadnezzar at Carchemish in 605. The latter rebuilt Babylon and revived its ancient glory, but his followers were weak and unable to face the new power which now arose. Babylon fell to Cyrus of Persia in 538 and at least for little Israel a new day had dawned.

Perhaps a word ought here to be added about Assyria in order to redress the imbalance in this story of unceasing plunder and devastation. The work of a pioneer is frought with perils, and out of all the nations upon earth Assyria was the first to feel the reins of real power. There was within her grasp the distinct possibility of a world empire. But there was no possibility of appeal to precedent, no guide from the past, and in mitigation of judgment this vital fact must be remembered. Yet Assyria did embark upon the task of organization and administration over a large area for the first time. As a martial race she has had but one rival, and if she had possessed rulers of the administrative skill of a Darius or an Alexander, the story might have been very different.

She has this merit: she carefully preserved the culture and religion of the Babylonians and passed on to posterity such inscriptions and works of art as have thrilled the hearts of Assyriologists all over the world.

PERSIA. 550–330 B.C.

The Character of the people. Although the Persians built up a massive well-governed empire, the greatest perhaps with the exception of Alexander's, they were not a warlike and aggressive people. Less cruel than the Assyrians, less superstitious than the Babylonians, and less flamboyant than the Greeks, the Persians possessed positive qualities which, in some respects, outshone them all. Assyria appeared cruel for cruelty's sake, Babylon fought to defend her prestige, Greece fought to banish the Barbarians, but Persia was almost reluctantly forced into the limelight. Rarely has a people so kindly, cultured and tolerant, been forced into a position of power. The Persians did not begin by seeking power. Without the aggressive thrust and the impetus of prestige which meant so much to her rivals, Persia moved slowly but certainly into a position of power. But having taken her place in the centre of the world's stage it took no less than an Alexander to dislodge her. Yet just because Persia was much more leisurely in inaugurating her campaigns she was able to give a great deal more thought to the planning of them. For the calmly calculated, carefully conceived, chess-like approach to the strategy of war, Persia takes the credit. Her military plans were copied by later conquerors, her method of building great highroads was copied with great advantage by the later Romans. The survival of Persia as a nation was partly due to Persian character and partly to the teachings of Zoroaster.

Persia has the credit of providing the most civilized empire in the ancient world. Her people were really more at home in the pursuit of peace than in the art of war. They were lovers of flowers and gave to the world roses, tulips and lilac. They were lovers of Truth, and even though there were lapses, their reverence for Truth and their objective approach to it show a highly-developed moral sense. They were lovers of animals, each Persian noble having his own 'paradise' where wild animals roamed at will. The Persian horse was the finest breed of the ancient world, and while the Persians were clever horsemen, it should be added that in this respect they owed much to the Assyrians. Animals were protected mainly for hunting purposes, however, and not from any great interest in zoology. They were lovers of money, and although there is nothing peculiar in this, they had the sense to issue imperial coinage which facilitated trade and brought increasing prosperity. It was wrong to be in debt, wrong to tell lies, wrong to dishonour the king, and it is interesting to notice that with these standards Persia survived as a nation when Babylon and Assyria were no more.

The phase of conquest. They taught their children an intense loyalty to the King, and there arose for the first time what might be described as the Divine Right of Kings. It is reported that Persian nobles were ready to jump overboard to lighten the ship when Xerxes, their King, was in danger at sea. But perhaps this was not entirely due to a sense of loyalty but to the strict discipline which was imposed by all Persian monarchs. The price of disobedience was too well known to be ignored. So while the Persians had many qualities, they lacked one thing which other nations have greatly prized—freedom. The people had no constitutional rights, and the social order, with the King at its head, was immune from criticism. The following incident gives some indication of the position: Wishing to marry his sister, Cambyses, son of Cyrus, called in the royal judges to enquire whether there was a law permitting this practice; the wise judges answered that they could find no such law, but they did find one "that the King of the Persians might do whatever he pleased." The truth of the story is attested by King Darius who had no desire either to alter or question it.

> *"Tis not in mortals to command success,*
> *But we'll do more, Sempronius, we'll deserve it."*

If any ancient king deserved success, it was Cyrus. The Persian stories about Cyrus (559–530 B.C.) are legendary, but even when they are stripped of all romanticism and patriotic eulogy, it remains true that he was an outstanding leader of men, a great soldier and a benevolent ruler. In war, he was a master tactician, in victory, a man who could temper justice with mercy. The example of personal courage played an important part in his victories. The story is told of Croesus, the Lydian King, who asked Cyrus to send a messenger to him to discuss terms of surrender. But Cyrus himself appeared with the words

"I am my own messenger." It was a day to be remembered; Cyrus threw down the gauntlet, turned his camels on the Lydian cavalry, and since that day, in desert lands the cavalry has been no match for camel regiments.

It took Cyrus and his son, Cambyses, twenty-five years to conquer Asia Minor, Babylon and Egypt. Part of their success was due to a new element which they introduced in their treatment of conquered enemies. They adopted a skilful policy of tempering their absolutism with clemency and generosity, and in this Cyrus was a pioneer. His treatment of Israel was in line with his general policy. Discarding the Assyrian method of crushing national cultures by brutality and deportation, he adopted the wiser and better method of allowing subject peoples to keep their own laws, religions, languages, and sometimes their own princes. This system was beneficial in two respects: it meant that national cultures were preserved to enrich the world, and that other rulers were given an example of clemency and of the responsibilities of their office. Eventually Cyrus was defeated by the Scythians when he was attacking Egypt. Cambyses continued the struggle in Egypt but fell on his sword while mounting his horse and Darius became king.

The phase of consolidation. When Darius came to the throne (521 B.C.) there were rebellions everywhere. Scarcely can a ruler have faced so many upheavals. There were revolts in Media, Elam, Armenia and Babylon, but in the end, his firm determination to win and his skill as a diplomat won the day. He won nineteen victories and became master of the most ancient kingdoms of the world. His empire included the region from Turkistan to the Persian Gulf, the Caucasus, Egypt, Palestine, Cyprus, Afghanistan and Baluchistan, so there is little wonder that he became known as an oriental king of kings.

How did he face the administrative problems of this great empire? He appointed twenty rulers to various parts of his empire and trained them for office. Great sums rolled into his treasury, and the palaces at Persepolis and Susa were the envy of the world. The Medes and Persians were, of course, exempt from taxation, but the provinces of empire paid heavily. Cilicia provided horses and Babylon provided silver, but the king was not satisfied with silver and introduced a gold coinage. Unlike the Greeks and the Phoenicians, the Persians had no great flair for trade, but their revenue was such that they hardly needed it. As a consequence of this Darius did much to develop banking, commerce and industry. When his work in establishing communications by building canals and roads, and his many legal reforms are added to his other achievements, it will be easy to see that in his day Persia reached the zenith of her power. But like many an ancient ruler he was not satisfied with mere consolidation, he wanted to extend his empire.

All through his life he had been spurred on by an ambition to conquer the Greeks, but when he faced them at Marathon (490 B.C.) his forces were completely routed, and before he could gather together his scattered forces, death intervened. It is only just to Darius to say that this event marked the beginning of the end for the Persian empire.

The phase of capitulation. Xerxes had by no means the qualities of Cyrus and Darius, and he was no match for the Greeks. He was defeated on the banks of the Eurymedon (466 B.C.) and was forced to leave Europe. The kings that followed, with the exception of Artaxerxes III (359–338), were weak and unable to rule with a strong hand. They lost no time in dissipating the vast resources which had been built up by Darius. Uninspired by any great cause, they revelled in luxurious living and this brought moral degeneration. Intrigue and bribery flourished and the provincial rulers took the law into their own hands. Egypt was always ready to assert her independence, and money was wasted in the futile attempt to keep her quiet. But the greatest reason for the decline of the Persian empire was their complete miscalculation regarding the growing power of the Greeks. Yet there had been several clear warnings: they had been defeated at Marathon, Salamis and Plataea, and still they had ignored the writing on the wall. Darius III came to the throne of Persia in the very same year that Alexander came to the throne of Macedon (336), and the former could not have dreamed that his destiny would be decided three years later at Issus. Two years later the whole of the Persian empire passed into the hands of the Greeks. Yet this must be said: even in the height of their power the Persian kings revealed qualities which are rarely associated with despotic rulers, and after all, Persia has survived as a national entity, and has given to the world a religion (Zoroastrianism) which claims its followers to this day

CHAPTER XII

GREEK HISTORY AND CULTURE

THE BACKWARD LOOK

Emerson begins his essay on History with the words: "Man is explicable by nothing less than all his history." At least in this chapter we go back to the beginning of recorded history. History is the human saga; it is not just observation but interpretation as well. It is explanation as well as description. It is not just a series of facts but a series of insights into facts. These facts are the result of human responses to given situations In some ages there have been all the makings of an immortal saga but no record of it. Sometimes there has been the record but only the record of events. But there can be no history without people. When there are great men living in the midst of small events history becomes dull and uninteresting. Hence Churchill's comment on the Victorian era: "How these Victorians busied themselves and contended about minor things! . . . Rosebery flourished in an age of great men and small events." Ancient Greece was fortunate, she was provided with great events, great personalities and great historians. It is the synchronization of these factors which makes the history of Greece a fascinating story.

India, for instance, has not produced any great school of historical writing, and at first it seems strange that a country rich in epic, lyric and philosophy should represent history as a blank. Yet it is hardly surprising when three factors are taken into account. There are long periods in the history of India which are still dark, and the reason for this is not far to seek. A nation's history depends to some extent upon contact with other races. Before Alexander we know little about India, but we hear something about it soon after his day. Again, when we consider Indian philosophy we shall see that this lack of historical interest and record is what we might have expected. History is myth for the Hindu, the visible world is 'maya,' illusion or unreality. It is no more stable than the changing panoramas of the clouds. When the idea of Karma is added to the above, we have a very distorted view of history. The past exists only to be forgotten, and the purpose of life is no more than the individual expiation of its evil deeds. It is true that an element of judgment is introduced but judgment for the sake of judgment is like a prison system without a state.

The Greeks, on the other hand, were not bedevilled by any Maya or Karma doctrine, and they produced men who were interested in history and wrote it and were indeed the pioneers of historical writing in the West. First among them was Herodotus (484–425 B.C.). He was well equipped for his work. Wide travel, careful observation, a love of truth, and the facility for recording his experiences, are essential qualifications for the historian. Herodotus possessed all these gifts. He was appalled by the neglect of history, and the realization of this which came to him on his travels provided the necessary impetus. He visited lands like Egypt and Persia which had been making history over a long period but had not taken the trouble to study or record it. Why was it that the amazing story of the life and development of a nation had not been recorded? His own work is part of the answer to that question. It is significant that it was a Greek, not a Persian, who first recorded the history of the Persian Empire.

Where events had been recorded, he found a one-sided picture. He noticed that the scribes in Egypt and Mesopotamia had recorded only the mighty deeds of kings, and no doubt there were good reasons why the scribes had not applied a critical faculty. There were glowing stories about the rule of the Pharaohs and the achievements of Assyrian conquerors but nothing about the daily life of the common people, their customs, labour, religion, inventions and pastimes.

He made it a part of his duty to separate fact from fiction, and while it must be admitted that he was not very successful in this, it was something to have made the attempt. Of course, we cannot expect that he should apply the laws of scientific enquiry and evidence as would a modern historian, yet it is remarkable that he, a great lover of Greece, was so objective and dispassionate in his observations concerning other nations. If curiosity and intelligence make a real historian, then Herodotus must be regarded not only as the first in time but the first in importance too. He drew interesting conclusions: "Every nation prefers its own customs," yet he would have been the first to admit that as a patriotic Greek he shared this tendency with the rest.

There were other striking conclusions: "There are laws which all men hold in common." It was the similarity of these laws which had evolved in many lands which first gave him the idea of a pattern in history. He quoted with approval Pindar's words: "Law is king over all."

In general his ideas of religion are those of his age, and he shared its fatalism. Although he had respect for the gods, and often resorted to the Delphic Oracle, he accepted the idea of an ultimate fate: "It is not possible even for a god to escape the decree of destiny." He maintained that one generation inevitably reaped the consequences of the previous one, but this collective interpretation is rather different from the individualistic concept which is implicit in the Karma theory. Yet after referring to these inevitable consequences he seems to find nothing inconsistent in saying that everything is due to the jealousy of the gods. What really impressed him was the fact that man was able to make reasonable progress in the world in spite of the jealousy of the gods. He had the greatest regard for human achievements and resourcefulness, and in the end he is convinced that history is a man-made story. The poet Alcaeus sums up his view:

> Now is the moment, now,
> To take what happiness the gods allow.

Although there is much more to praise than to blame in the work of Herodotus, we must draw attention to two weaknesses. He did not make a clear enough distinction between fact and fiction. When we see an oriental film, especially one with a Hindu background, it is impossible to tell whether the scene is supposed to be staged in heaven or on earth. The gods flit to and fro, sometimes on Mount Kailas which is heaven, and sometimes on the plains of earth. But the scenery of earth is so lavish and elaborate that we are never quite sure where we are. Some of the records of Herodotus are like an oriental film. The truth is not easily separated from the myth. It is true that he used to tell his hearers that he did not necessarily believe the tales he had heard and recorded, but his manner of telling them often persuaded them of their truth. Sometimes, therefore, the light he gave led them astray.

He was not altogether to blame for this. In those days a student listened to history narrated. It was a sort of romantic story which was told for its entertainment value. Long before the stories of Herodotus were recorded, he had no doubt told them in public. These were great occasions and Herodotus had perfected the art of relating history through tales. It may be that because the tale had to be entertaining the truth sometimes was sacrificed. Nevertheless he did a good day's work not only for Greece but for all the world and we are in his debt.

THE INWARD LOOK

If Herodotus looked back, Homer looked within. It has been observed that in later life Beethoven became so deaf that he never physically heard his own greatest compositions. He continued to compose. This may not mean 'creation out of nothing' but it is very near to it. His music was not a variation of someone else's theme, it was the result of the muse, it was music from within. Similarly there was poetry in Homer's soul. He looked within because outwardly there was nowhere to look. That is to say Homer had no great poetic predecessor. Not only did he set the pace, he was the first to do so; not only did he write poetry, he invented it; not only did his work inspire his own age, it set a pattern for posterity, and all who have followed in making story-poems owe something to Homer.

Despite the words in Ecclesiastes "There is nothing new under the sun," in Homer's time poetry was new. But his greatness does not solely rest on the fact that he was the original poet, but also on the fact that he was able to accomplish so much with a second-rate theme. It must be confessed that the plot of the Iliad is not very promising. It is the story of Achilles who sat in his tent offended, angry and disgruntled because of a quarrel with Agamemnon. It is a small and depressing theme. But the astonishing imagination of Homer weaves around it such varied patterns of romance, adventure and heroism, that he succeeds in making a dull episode into an immortal epic. There lies his genius, the ability to find so much challenge and inspiration in a minor event. He might have based his epic on a greater and grander theme—the defeat of Troy. Instead he chose the dark forebodings in the mind of a temperamental hero. It follows that the Iliad becomes a psychological study of the moods and attitudes of one man, Achilles. This is a major characteristic of this epic: attention is focussed on the mind of a man rather than on a series of events. On the whole, man is seen to transcend events.

The Odyssey emphasizes this more than the Iliad. In it there is less war and more tranquillity, less violence and more character, less illusion and more reality, less aimlessness and more purpose, less static moodiness and more dynamic action. Here again we have the story of the adventures of a man's mind. Never has a story enshrined and revealed so much human excellence and glory. What is the secret behind Ulysses, the warrior-genius? On this question Homer leaves us in no doubt. Ulysses possessed an unconquerable soul, an understanding mind, and an indomitable will. These qualities enabled him to face all obstacles, solve all problems, defeat all enemies, and ultimately arrive back in Athaca. It is Ulysses who suggests the stratagem of the wooden horse, an unlikely story since the Trojans were not likely to be easily duped, but at least it shows that the mind of man may conceive ways and means of overcoming the most impregnable barriers. Where violence fails, the wit of man succeeds. The Cyclopean episode illustrates the same truth. Cyclops had been blinded but still he stood astride the exit from the vast cave. Violence was no use here, for he was more than a match for his captives. So they donned sheep-skins and crept on all fours, and he let them pass, all of them. So when everything else fails, the mind finds a way.

Homer brought to his task a lively imagination, and with this faculty he gave to the great deeds of the past an even greater splendour. It is true that he was writing about an heroic age, but his imagination turned heroes into supermen. Yet it was not imagination alone which produced the great epics, it was imagination plus inspiration. It was this element in his work which stamped the culture of Greece and made Aeschylus describe his own plays as "slices from the great banquet of Homer." For Homer was greater than the world of which he wrote and enriched it with the qualities and ideals of his own mind. Yet perhaps even these great ideals were not entirely his own. He was not simply a man devising a fable and casting around for the best method of communicating it. There was a deeper reason: a vision of life had been disclosed to him and the content of his vision dictated the manner and method of its communication. Something controlled him and he became the willing instrument for the transmission of his vision. He was a true poet.

His work is infused with moral ideals which are far in advance of the world about which he wrote. He was not interested in bravado for its own sake, and if sometimes the very human Homer looked over his shoulder to judge the possible reactions of his audience, it is always the deeper and lasting message which shines through. And what is his message? That the ideal of honour is more important than victory; that the good life matters more than the long life; that the courageous spirit is more important than the achievement. Moreover his work is not characterized by the pessimism, cynicism and fatalism which marred the life of his own age. He is really teaching his people how to live well and how to die well.

His message, however, is incidental. It is unlikely that he was conscious of a moral aim. He did not set out to enlighten but to entertain. There are times when he hints at the motive behind his writings: he sings because he must. He writes for the joy of writing. In the eighth book of the Odyssey, King Alcinous gives orders for the entertainment of Ulysses by means of the customary story, song and dance. Was Homer unwittingly giving us the reason for his own song?

> Now did the herald approach and the clear-toned
>   lute that he carried
> Give to the blind old singer, who stepp'd to
>   the midst—and around him
> Boys in the bloom of their youth took stand
>   right skilful in dancing;
> So with a wonderful measure they smote on
>   the ground, and Odysseus
> Gazed at the flash and the twinkle of feet, and
>   he marvelled in spirit.

Then to his lute uplifting his beautiful voice
    did the singer
Sing of the passion of Ares for fair-crowned
    Queen Aphrodite.

But whether or not he was consciously delivering a message to mankind, his work rings true, and this is important from a literary as well as an ethical point of view. His heroes, once delineated, run true to form, and this consistency is a remarkable literary feat. The ideas of Achilles, and even more his character, are not suddenly changed, but his somewhat sulky and vexed attitude remains throughout. Even when he is moved to an heroic deed like the challenge to Hector, he is prompted by the desire to avenge the death of his friend, and we are made aware that the theme of his injured pride is still there.

Nor should we overlook the realism of the epics. Everything is brought out into the clear light of day. He has no concept of the later esoteric gnosis, nothing is left hidden or obscure. He is not writing of shadows and phantoms, his characters are real and clearly defined. He provides us with an open sesame, withholding nothing. And if after all their exploits and experiences, Achilles in the Iliad and Ulysses in the Odyssey are exactly the same men that we knew at the beginning, no better and no worse, this is at least typical of the static and horizontal attitude to life which characterized Greek drama. If characters of fine gold do not emerge after they have passed through the fires, at least they are no worse and certainly they have not been tainted by the experience. Such stark realism always surprises, but somehow it satisfies as well.

His work remains to inspire, and perhaps that is the supreme test of its value. de Burgh gives three reasons for the significance of the epics for later civilization: "Their beauty and splendour have been a perennial source of poetic inspiration; (they) came to be read and taught as a storehouse of moral and religious truth; and these poems have a value for history. They depict with substantial fidelity the life of the chieftains and warriors of the Aegean world in the later centuries of the second millenium." Let it stand, it is a fair verdict.

THE FORWARD LOOK

Not for a hundred and fifty years had Athens known a man of the intellectual and statesmanlike quality of Pericles (490–429). Solon had undoubtedly laid the foundations of Athenian democracy but Pericles inaugurated reforms which Solon dare not have attempted. The character and achievements of Pericles are altogether remarkable. Taught by Zeno and Anaxagorus he was brilliantly endowed, being a great

statesman, a great soldier and a great orator. These gifts alone would
have assured him of the leadership of Athens but he had other accomplishments; he was an artist, a philosopher and city-builder as well.
The impact of his amazing career may be estimated by the single fact
that his name was used to describe the most brilliant epoch the world
has ever seen. Although reserved and having no desire for power he was
called to be democratic leader in 461 and for the next twenty years
became the chief director of affairs.

He was an outstanding orator and his favourite theme was the glory
of Athens. The following speech, even after translation, is both moving
and arresting. Following the pattern of many of his speeches he combines the appeal to history with the challenge of the present: "I would
have you day by day fix your eyes on the greatness of Athens until you
become filled with the love of her; and when you are impressed by the
spectacle of her glory, reflect that this empire has been acquired by men
who knew their duty and had the courage to do it; who in the hour of
conflict, had the fear of dishonour always present to them; and who, if
they ever failed in an enterprise, would not allow their virtue to be lost
to their country, but freely gave of their lives to her as the fairest offering
they could present at her feet."

Needless to say he used his oratory in the service of his statesmanship.
He began by depriving the Aristocratic Party of the chief instrument of
its power—the Areopagus. Ever since the days of Solon all power had
been invested in this select body of rulers. But Pericles began the
process of de-centralization. Magistrates were now elected by lot so that
wealth and status were no longer the deciding factors. The poorest man
in Athens had an equal chance of election with all the rest. The judicial
powers of the Senate of Five Hundred were abolished and paid jury-
courts were appointed. These courts were open to men of all classes
and trades. But even more important than all this was the fact that the
standard of public life was raised and a new respect for law and new
principles of integrity were infused into the life of the state. Pericles
was determined to make Athens a free city, a rich city, a city cultured
and self-governing. The first of these was an attempt to break the
long-standing parochialism of the city-state, while the last, by investing
civic responsibility in every citizen, meant an all-out effort for the good
of the state. Of the other two aims, one secured the continuing progress
of Athens, and the other—Athenian culture—has become a by-word in
the whole civilized world.

It is not to be supposed that such a programme could be implemented
without opposition from other states. In order to offset this, Pericles
aimed at strengthening the link with continental Greece, and succeeded
in forming alliances with Thessaly, Argos and Megara. His system of

colonization furthered this effort. Certain lands in the colonies were claimed for the exclusive use of Athenians who were allowed to live there while retaining their citizenship. But difficulties arose: even some of his independent allies revolted. They resented the high taxation exacted by Athens and the transference of all lawsuits to Athens. Pericles himself sailed against the Samians in 440 and defeated them, but he was less successful against the Corinthians five years later.

Nevertheless Periclean Athens stands as one of the great achievements of creative power. Equally important is the astonishing influence upon others in later ages. In almost every department of learning men go back to drink at the springs of Hellas.

> *Her citizens, imperial spirits,*
> *Rule the present from the past,*
> *On all this world of men inherits,*
> *Their seal is set.*

It is sometimes suggested that if the Athenian Confederacy had not been torn by inter-state war, and later by the long drawn-out conflict with Persia, the Athenians would have exerted an even greater influence upon the world. The case is hard to prove, for Athens has dominated western thought in spite of her problems and conflicts. Some of the reasons for her primacy are seen when her manner of life is compared with that of Sparta, her nearest rival. The poet Simonides had said: "The city is the teacher of the man," and this gives a clue to her genius. Athens sought knowledge, Sparta sought strength. Sparta has become synonymous with a tough and disciplined life and with physical prowess; Athens was more interested in cultural power. Yet the tough, disciplined regime in Sparta contained a cruel streak, and often lame children and twin girls were left to die of exposure in the jungles. It is useless to argue in defence of Sparta that such practices were typical of that age; they were not typical of life in Athens. The Athenians must have known of them but were not influenced by them. Sparta was a totalitarian state while Athens was a free city. In Sparta theft was introduced into the strategems of war, in Athens it was a serious crime. Spartan boys were taught that it was immodest to speak in the presence of their elders, in Athens the streets were filled with young folk eagerly questioning the philosophers. In some ways Sparta represents a prison, a corrective training camp, while Athens was almost a continuous academic festival. In the end the influence of Athens survived, not because she was stronger than Sparta but because in every aspect of life she had the forward look.

This forward look is noticeable in Athenian art as well. Until the seventh century art was generally uninteresting and ossified. It was limited by certain stylistic fixations. It simply reproduced the same old ideas, and introduced nothing which might have made Greek art a living issue. They now tried to be more realistic, thinking in terms of movement and of living forms. The increase of wealth made sculpture possible and the same dynamism was applied to that also. Sculpture became the expression of Greek thought. Phideas (438) had been working on a statue of Athene, and when asked about his model, quoted Homer:

> *Zeus spoke, and speaking his dark brows unclosed,*
> *The ambrosial locks from that immortal head*
> *Streamed, and made the great Olympus shake.*

Detailed attention was given to the construction of temples. But it should be remembered that the Greek temple was essentially a house for god and not a place for congregations. There was no need for a large interioi, and the architects and sculptors concentrated on the external proportions. It follows that unnecessary decorations or elaborations were excluded. These also depict the forward look; they were strong, majestic, durable structures. Many of these temples remain.

The city-state for all its glory, could not last. Partly because no nation can survive in the face of continuous civil strife; partly because Athenian culture was too great to be cribbed and cabined in Athens alone; and partly because the national ideal was a greater one, and in any case this alone could ensure the security of the Greek nation as a whole. The quarrels between Athens and Sparta continued until 405 when Athens was razed to the ground, and although she revived she was too exhausted to withstand the might of a new conqueror, Philip of Macedon. Philip soon became the master of the whole Hellenic world (338), but two years later he was murdered and it was left to his son and successor, Alexander, to show what a united Greece could do; he went out to conquer the East but it turned out to be a conquest of Greek culture as well as an example of Greek courage.

THE UPWARD LOOK

It was never easy for the Greeks to look upward in hope. Although the eyes of the Greeks were always on 'to kalon' (the Good and the Beautiful), their bright visions were prevented from being realized because of their innate pessimism. Their eyes might scan the far off horizons yet the iron ball of fate checked all progress. The Deity beckoned but the iron hand of Destiny held them back. A gloom overshadowed all their enterprises. Yet it must be confessed that this gloom concerned the present rather than the future. What happened after death did not greatly trouble the Greeks, they were creatures of the day and lived for the day. They were keen lovers of life, looking for and rejoicing in new sensations and new experiences. They were full of zest for life and wanted to be happy on earth. That they were pre-eminently concerned with history as 'this life' is manifested in their whole civilization and culture. In order to live this life happily and effectively they needed constant inspiration and for this they looked to the Good and the Beautiful. There is a wistfulness in their search for truth, a feeling that Reality is meant to be found, and that Reality is more important than illusion and more lasting than falsehood. The Greeks always wanted to reach the stars, although too often the stars appeared to recede. Why did this happen? That was the question that puzzled them, and this feeling of frustration and defeat coloured much of their thinking. After the appalling tragedy of the death of Heracles, Sophocles writes:

> *You have seen strange things,*
> *Unheard of sufferings,*
> *And all that you have seen is Zeus.*

Even here there is the feeling that he would have liked things to have been different. If only sometimes Zeus had been associated with hope and joy instead of darkness and sorrow! Biting irony expressed a strong protest against things as they were:

"In politics, the powerful exact what they can, and the weak grant what they must." Yet such frustration often quickened the search for truth, and in this search they were helped by a great language from whose rich storehouse and resourcefulness they drew constant inspiration. This enabled them to go straight to the point and say with clarity what had to be said. Their contemporaries in China were content to fulfil their traditional rites, content also to face many a crisis by the strength of family piety; and for the Buddhists, who were spreading their way of life in India, detachment was the price of serenity. This was not the case with the Greeks; their intellectual drive was too strong for contentment and too persistent for detachment. They seized upon all the facts of experience and investigated the entire moral and physical order of the world.

> *The unaging order*
> *Of deathless nature,*
> *Of what is it made, and whence, and how?*

It must be confessed, however, that although the Greeks looked upward in hope they were always looking through a cloud. They were too conscious of the hand of fate and too oppressed by chance and accident. The writing of the 'moving finger' could never be erased, and the writing on the wall was invariably a message of doom. There is a tragic finality at the end of the Iliad: "That was the funeral of Hector." That is how it all ends, that is how all things end, "not with a bang but a whimper." There is bitterness, cynicism and despair in many of their writings, and we look in vain for a word of joy or a ray of hope.

"Child, be not over-distressed, no man is immortal." Life was brief and it was rounded off by a brief time of mourning, and therefore it was better not to take things too seriously. Although life was brief, it was unrelieved sorrow: "Never by day shall they rest from travail and sorrow, and never by night from the hand of the Spoiler" (Hesiod). It was this complete absence of purpose, the sheer futility and meaningless of existence which oppressed them most: "Not to be born is the best thing in the world, and failing that, to die as quickly as possible and fade away into nothingness." Such is the verdict of Sopholcles. The cynicism of the following lines have rarely been surpassed:

Here lie I, Dionysius of Tarsus, sixty years old, unwed;
Would that my father had been the same.

Life was cyclic and in the end this resulted in a static concept of existence. Man strove endlessly only to find himself where he began. Parmenides says: "It is all one to me when I begin, for I shall come back again there." The words of Heraclitus imply the same truth: "All things are passing, both human and divine, upwards and downwards by exchanges." But is there any sense or reason in a wheel of life which turns full circle and brings us back to the place where we began? No wonder the Greeks were sad.

One thing alone surpasses the pessimism of the Greek, it is his courage. He was ready to brush aside all his sorrows and try again. So the Stoic sings: "Thou mayest save me, thou mayest sink me if thou wilt, but I'll keep my rudder true." And Seneca's boatman left a message among the rocks:

A shipwrecked sailor bids you here set sail,
For many a gallant barque went on and beat the gale.

Even in his last moments Hector does not lose courage; facing Achilles he says: "Now then, death is near me, there can be no delay, there is no escape . . . Yet I pray that I may die not without a blow, not inglorious."

Perhaps it was inevitable that if they continued to look upward, even if they looked through a cloud, someone would one day see beyond the cloud to the sunlit hills where the gods might be. Homer was a visionary as well as a poet. If he did not make the Olympians he certainly made their reputation. He gave them a local habitation and a name. They lived on Mount Olympus; the sky god was Zeus, the nature goddess—Athene, the sea god—Poseidon, and the fertility goddess—Aphrodite. There were many others too and each god and goddess was given a name and a nature and a home. Homer has this merit: he changed the Olympians from vague and shapeless ideals to clearly-defined characters.

Yet the Olympians bear all the marks of human invention. Perhaps

Homer's work was to crystallize Greek thought about the objects of worship. The Olympians are idealized thoughts, reflections of human behaviour. They therefore emerge as glorified human beings, Apollo is a model of manhood, Zeus a sort of feudal overlord, and Aphrodite the symbol of an old fertility cult. They provide a focus for human desires and aspirations but scarcely qualify to be revered as objects of worship. They are gods from 'this side' rather than the 'other side.' They do not provide any new revelation from the Beyond. Perhaps the Greeks did not expect this, for the more human their gods, the more they loved them.

But all this means, of course, that the Olympians are cast in a minor role. They feasted, laughed, slept, made love, and as long as the gods were preoccupied with these pursuits, their worshippers had little to fear. The Greeks were happy when the gods were busy. It is true that sometimes the gods showed themselves to be angry and vindictive, but perhaps these stories of anger and violence were related for the benefit of the enemies of Greece. On the whole the gods were pleasant but powerless, genial but pathetic. They were neither makers nor rulers of the world and in no sense did they accept responsibility for it. Even as examples of the good life, they fall short and there is no suggestion that holiness and immortality are in their power to bestow. Sophocles and Xenophanes discarded the Olympian gods altogether, and the historian Thucydides in his attack upon religion in general does not even mention them: "When visible grounds of confidence forsake them, some have recourse to the invisible, to prophecies, oracles and the like. These ruin men by the hopes they inspire in them."

There are certain questions which arise in connection with any polytheistic system, and unfortunately the Greeks made no attempt to answer them. How is it possible to please many gods? Can there be a true relationship with gods who frequently change character? Whose guidance are the worshippers to follow and who has the prior claim to their obedience? But the greatest single drawback is that such gods give no specific directions about questions of morals and ethics. On these all-important questions the Olympians are dumb.

In the end, the Olympians are the strongest testimony to the fact of Greek self-sufficiency. The truth is that the Greeks exercised such initiative and enterprise and vigour in all the ordinary affairs of life that they appeared to have little need of the Olympians. They liked to know the gods were there and they undoubtedly wanted their enemies to know it, but this is purely a defence mechanism and does not deserve the name of religion. Homer himself was partly responsible for this casual attitude for he showed less respect for the gods than for his heroes.

Professor Gilbert Murray has pointed out that Olympian religion resulted in two notable achievements: it debarbarized the worship of the leading states of Greece, and it worked for concord and fellow-feeling throughout the Greek communities. But while recognizing Homer's contribution in this respect, it is necessary to say that in no sense had Olympianism the makings of a permanent religious Faith. Eventually the gods vanished in the mists of Olympus, and this was partly due to the coming of Plato, and even more to the coming of Christ whose advent effectively checked any hope of their reappearance.

CHAPTER XIII

THE MINOR EMPIRES OF THE NEAR EAST

SUMER AND AKKAD

Measured against giants like Babylon, Assyria, Persia and Greece, the empires we shall now consider may, perhaps, be regarded as minor ones. Yet when their achievements are remembered it is hard to think of them in terms of a minor role. In 4500 B.C. Mesopotamia was divided into two separate countries, Sumer and Akkad. The Sumerians lived in the south and the Akkadians in the north. The Akkadians were semitic, while the Sumerians were non-semitic. The Akkadians probably came from Arabia, and the Sumerians originated in the East. It is generally agreed that the Sumerians shaped Babylonian civilization.

From them we have received our earliest information about the religions of mankind. A people so far advanced as to live in an organized society, to create good architecture, excellent pottery and a written script, cannot easily be dismissed with the term 'primitive culture.' Long before Greece and Rome appeared as centres of culture and power, there were three areas which seemed to flower almost simultaneously into an advanced civilization. These were Mesopotamia, Egypt and India. If the contribution of the Sumerians to civilization has sometimes been underrated, it is largely because the spectacular flash with which they burst upon the world has seemed almost unbelievable. Some have regarded it as a flash in the pan, but this is to misrepresent the case. Any nation which begins by draining the whole country, building cities even with mud walls, and writing inscriptions on clay, deserves to be remembered and honoured in history. Some examples of their inventiveness may be mentioned.

The first was the use of beasts for power to replace human muscles alone. This was applied in two directions, for ploughing the land and for transport. At that time land was dug with a digging stick or a hoe, but if you can get an ox to draw a big hoe, you do not only cultivate more ground but you cultivate it deeper and more effectively, and this brings an increase in the amount of food one worker can produce.

This leads to another development. If you can get an ox to draw a cart, you can carry extra food from farm to city and by taking advantage of this easy form of transport, you can save time and human energy.

But all this depends to a large extent upon another vital discovery—that of the wheel. Oxen were in fact used to drag dry-land sledges before wheels were invented. It is interesting to note that carts and war chariots drawn by oxen or donkeys (horses were not yet used), appeared before 3000 B.C. But the wheel was used not only for transport, but also to speed up pottery making. Its uses were manifold: the Romans used it later to control central heating in the public baths, and the prayer wheel was in use in India five hundred years before the Buddha.

Another great advance was in metal-working. In casting copper the Sumerians used the lost wax method. They made the desired object in wax, enclosed it in clay, and by baking it, hardened the clay and melted the wax at the same time. This left a hollow mould to receive the metal. Black sand has now become a substitute for clay, but the general Sumerian principle still holds good in moulding shops everywhere.

Also before 3000 B.C. it became known that by adding 10–15% of tin to copper, it was possible to produce bronze, and as this was not only easier to cast but tougher when it was finished, bronze rather than copper alone became man's chief industrial metal for a long period. Now it may be argued that metal for tools, and the plough and the wheel are not essential for an emergent civilization because, in fact, some races (e.g. the Mexicans) managed without them, but it must be said that these inventions worked miracles in the Middle East. They opened up paths of trade, produced more food, increased the prestige of the people, and, of course, increased their striking power, for knives and swords were sharper and stronger. When we add to the above achievements the fact that they introduced formal education, a system of credit, as well as providing the first weights and measures, we shall realize how great is the world's debt to the Sumerians.

Their thoughts about religion were becoming clearer and the gods became more and more important. At Erech there was the cult of Anu, the god of heaven and father of all gods; at Nippur, the cult Enlil, the earth-god; and at Kish, the cult of the earth-mother, Astarte. Some scholars have tried to find primitive monotheism in Sumerian religion, but they have a hard task because it is well known that there were over 500 gods in the ancient Sumerian pantheon. Their interest in religion is indicated by the building of elaborate temples in the cities. They began to use glazed bricks to build great arches, and this was followed by the construction of pyramids and towers of Babel (3000–2500 B.C.) which called for a knowledge of mathematics as well as building techniques.

The temples began to show a marked richness in precious objects and gold, and in ornamentation and glazed bricks. This shows that such buildings had already become the focus of society. Great wealth was invested in these temples, and the gods ruled the people through the priests. As in parts of India today the temples formed a sort of corporation which owned and rented out much of the land and collected taxes. So the priesthood and the gods were the nerve centre around which city life was formed. Of course, many Cistercian monasteries in the 11th and 12th centuries in this country functioned in a similar way. In short, the temples of Sumer and Akkad were in control of politics and economics as well as religion. Trade meant accounts and the first recorded accounts go back to 3300 B.C. It is clear that they dealt with all sorts of loans, rentals of land, and estimates of labour. The results of their industrial inventions, their system of commerce, and indeed their gods were borrowed by the Babylonians and Assyrians. In about 2000 B.C. the Amorites (Amurru) settled in the northern cities and eventually made Babylon their capital. A new empire with a more centralized form of government began to emerge, and the names Sumer and Akkad which had added so much to the stock of human invention and enterprise began to fade, but their influence remains.

THE HITTITES

While we receive the impression in the Old Testament that the Hittites were a local tribe which was sometimes a nuisance to the Israelites, we now know that such a notion grossly underestimates Hittite influence and power. From 1750–1250 B.C. they were masters of an empire of considerable size. They were Indo-European in origin and settled in Anatolia in the course of the third millennium. In 1600 they conquered Babylon and became the greatest power in the Near East. Their empire eventually stretched from Anatolia to Syro-Phoenicia. Theirs was a brutal civilization, and perhaps this was due to the harsh nature of the country in which they lived. Sternness was the hallmark of Hittite art and this again may be due to their geographical location. The raw material for the sculptors was basalt and this is the least rewarding of stones. At all events the images of gods they carved out of it were monstrosities calculated to inspire terror in their worshippers. Their religion was syncretistic and included divinities from Egypt, Syria and Phoenicia. But their two principle objects of worship were Teshub, the weather god, and Inanna, Queen of Heaven and Earth.

The Hittites will be remembered for one important reason: they sowed the seeds of democracy. Their cities were organized on the basis of a tribal democracy along the lines of the Greek City-States which they anticipated by 2000 years. The rulers were not boastful and despotic but shared their authority with a council of warriors. An interesting light on their character is revealed by the fact that they intimated their grievances to an enemy before attacking, and after they had won, adopted a more humane policy towards the conquered than any of their contemporaries. In this respect the Persians learned something from the Hittites.

The Hittites also produced a new sort of narrative prose. The king was expected to treat his warriors as equals and he had to explain and defend his actions in their presence. Thus King Hattusilis speaks to his assembly: "Lo I feel sick. I had presented to you the young Labarnas as him who should sit upon the throne: I the king, called him my son, I embraced him, I exalted him, I cared for him without a break. But he proved himself a young man not worth looking upon. He did not shed tears, he did not sympathize, he is cold and heartless. Then I, the king, called him and made him come to my bedside. No longer could I go on treating a nephew as a son." Myrsilis and others who followed adopted the same style. But this speech is important not only because it indicates a democratic outlook, and also shows the tender and kindlier side of the Hittite character, but because it reveals a singular failure in an otherwise sound system. The Hittites were never able to solve the problem of succession to the throne. Perhaps the system prevented any powerful ruler emerging, or perhaps no ruler had sufficient authority to name his successor. Nevertheless it was an interesting experiment in democratic rule, and even though there was a long road to travel before the idea received wide acceptance, the Hittites take the credit for making a beginning.

THE PHOENICIANS

The Phoenicians were the greatest sea-power of the ancient world. Geographically they were fortunate. They came to be known as the great distributors of the Middle East. Phoenicia was no match for some of the great powers, for although she had timber in abundance, she had no minerals. Yet the great powers could not do very much without her assistance. They depended upon Phoenicia for their export trade and for harbour facilities. Although blessed with many great ports like Tyre, Sidon, Beirut and Byblos, she was hemmed in by the mountains of Lebanon and had little hope of becoming a land power. The people of such a coastal strip might easily have sunk into mediocrity. If they were prevented by the terrain from moving inland, they could venture out to sea. This decision made them the first great maritime power. Tyre became the most important trading centre on the Mediterranean coast. King Solomon was dependent upon the ship-builders and sailors of Phoenicia, and without them he could not have amassed his fabulous wealth or secured the materials for the building of the temple.

Two of their great achievements are connected with their position as a maritime power. They were able to move farther afield than other races and their discovery of silver in Spain, and the wealth that inevitably followed, ensured them a strong position in the councils of the nations. The other achievement was the invention of the famous purple dye which they extracted from shell-fish. But the Phoenicians had another claim to fame. They invented the alphabet. The people of Byblos produced 22 signs, written in an original, clear and convenient script. At last there was a fixed alphabet, and reliable signs could be used to meet any situation. There is no need to stress how important was this development in the history of mankind. The alphabet was adopted by the Greeks, passed on to the Latins who transmitted it to the whole of the Western World.

The Phoenicians had two principal gods, El and Baal. The god El had his abode in a field, and, not surprisingly, his consort was Ashera of the Sea. El was the supreme over all other gods, but he had many opponents, the foremost of whom was Baal. El's son Mot, and Baal's son Aleion, were engaged in a continuous struggle for power. The life of the world, not only of men but of gods also, was bound up with the deaths and resurrections of Mot and Aleion. Ultimately the conqueror was Aleion, the son of Baal. All this was part of the crude polytheistic system which is by no means exaggerated in the pages of the Old Testament.

It is necessary to pause for a moment and survey what has happened lest we should miss the abiding significance of those momentous centuries. The setting down of these facts in this cold and objective fashion tends to make us overlook the imaginative quests and exciting inventions which characterized one of the great creative epochs in the story of man. The plough, the wheel, the alphabet, the beginnings of education, of democracy, of irrigation, of the moulding industry, the use of purple dye, the opening up of trade routes and the extension of the world's frontiers—all these in different ways have shaped the literature, commerce and industry of all succeeding centuries. It does not minimize the glory of these achievements when it is argued that such new ideas would have come to fruition sometime in any case. These things happened over four thousand years ago because enquiring and ingenious people opened up to the world their treasures of thought and invention. We owe all this as much to their perseverance and energy as to their observation and experiment. In short, they did these things because of the kind of people they were.

They were not primarily interested in feats of war. They applied their minds more to the arts of peace than to the ways of war. They were more interested in culture than in conquest. They sought the good of mankind rather than anything else. Their preoccupations were not those which we associate with later conquerors, they were learning how to live, how to read and write, how to think and create. And perhaps because they were minor empires they were able to make a contribution to civilization which the more powerful martial races could never give. Nothing can detract from their glorious achievement. Perhaps it is providential that in those early ages people existed whose creative genius and pacific temperament were to make such a difference to the life of man in later times. They gave time and interest and energy, and even though they were unconscious of it, the result of their labours is their legacy to the world. So as we consider how the story unfolds in the history of such mighty empires as Babylon, Assyria, Persia, Greece and Rome, we should not forget the important if less spectacular accomplishments of Sumer and Akkad, of the Hittites and Phoenicians.

CHAPTER XIV

ALEXANDER THE GREAT (356–323 B.C.)

THE MAN

Alexander had two great teachers, his father, Philip of Macedon, and Aristotle, one of the greatest of Greek Philosophers. The first trained him to be a leader in battle, the second taught him how to be a leader of thought. He was twenty years of age when his father was murdered. He found himself surrounded by a rebellious people and disgruntled generals. But those who patronizingly called him 'a mere boy' were soon to discover their mistake. Alexander was soon to prove himself the greatest strategist of all time. No Roman Caesar had greater tactical skill and no Persian monarch had his gift of consolidating his victories. His attitude in dealing with his victims was often merciful. He was not only a conqueror of enemies but a builder of states. He did not, as is sometimes supposed, revel in romantic campaigns, his work as a military leader was a necessity. He also possessed gifts which his father lacked. Philip, for all his victories and gold mines, died in debt. His armies had been too expensive to maintain. Alexander resolved to make his conquests pay for themselves.

THE CONQUEROR

As he swept into Asia, it seemed that nothing could stop him. He had all those capacities that go to make an incomparable military leader: ambition, technical skill, horsemanship and indomitable courage. Although resolute in battle, he was not cruel or vindictive to the conquered. The list of principal victories is worth noting: in 334 he over-ran Asia Minor, in 333 he routed the Persian King in Syria, two years later he defeated a huge Persian Army east of the Tigris and occupied the Persian homeland after fighting his way through the mountains in mid-winter. In 327 we find him conquering parts of India. He had hoped to cross India and reach the eastern sea-board, but his troops were weary, and having won a great victory over an army which included two hundred elephants, they refused to go any farther than the Ganges. In 325 he returned to Babylon, which he had made his temporary headquarters, but not before he had conducted the most spectacular military campaign ever known.

THE SCHOLAR

He was interested in culture as well as conquest. He was great even in a great race. He may be called a liberal scholar, refusing to be shackled by tradition or nationalism, and in some ways becoming the first internationalist. Although interested in the government of states and peoples, he also sought knowledge about the Ruler of the universe. One of his great gifts was the ability to rouse enthusiasm and idealism in others. Many of the stories about him are legendary but they all reflect his hold on the mind and imagination of his people. Even when we bear in mind his egoism and his insatiable thirst for conquest, we still have to ask how he managed to win widespread fame in spite of these human weaknesses. It was not simply the love of fighting which stirred him, he had three great desires: to bring glory to Greece, to widen his own knowledge, and to unify the nations that he conquered.

THE POLITICIAN

The greatness of Greece was mainly in her legacy to the world and especially to western civilization. In the sphere of government, she gave to the world democracy; in the sphere of learning, science and philosophy; in the sphere of architecture, Athens; in the sphere of commerce, Alexandria; and in the sphere of religion, the Alexandrine Schools and the Nicene Creed. Although it cannot be said that all this may be attributed to Alexander, it can be said that the Hellenizing movement began with him. The fact that he treated the Hindus as equals won their hearts and they were ready to acclaim him King of Asia. But this had a richer significance: it meant a merging of Oriental and Hellenic thought, a formidable combination, which began to leaven the thinking of many nations. By his defeat of the Persians he took the famous title, King of Kings, but to make assurance doubly sure he married Statira, daughter of Darius and thus united the two peoples. It is said that some of his officers and more than ten thousand of his soldiers followed his example and married Persian women. As a political move this was of the greatest importance, minimizing the possibility of rebellion and strengthening Alexander's grip on Persia.

In the end there are three ways of dealing with the culture of a conquered people, the conqueror may banish it altogether which is what Nebuchadnezzar tried to do with the culture of the Hebrews; or he may allow freedom of thought and religion while still retaining political rule, or he may accept and respect the culture of the conquered people and seek to re-shape it according to his own ideas. Alexander chose the third, and he had to be a skilled politician to bring it to success.

THE VISIONARY

Alexander was a man whose ideas were greater than his achievements, and his achievements were considerable. As victory followed victory a new view of the world began to take shape in his mind. If he had visions of world conquest, he had visions of world unity as well. He thought in terms of a world-wide kingdom but it must be a kingdom ruled wisely and justly, and he had much to teach his contemporaries on that point. He saw infinite possibilities for good in unity between Greek and Jew, Greek and Egyptian, Greek and Hindu, and partly through his vision and resolution, some of these possibilities soon became facts. The first union produced the Septuagint, the second produced the city of Alexandria, and the third enriched Greek Thought. Far more than his conquests, this intermingling of cultures influenced the civilizations of the world. He sought not to found an empire but to re-shape the world.

Soon after his death the empire was broken up and it is sad to say that the bickerings of incompetent leaders brought about its disintegration. For all his military skill he gave to the world deeper insights than the use of the sword. His plans and dreams show that in the end the mind is greater than the hand, and that while strength may prepare the way, it is Thought that claims the ultimate victory. Unity and peace are the result of enlightenment and not of war.

New ideas of citizenship followed. Until Alexander's appearance the Greeks had concentrated on the city-state, and while this was all right for a time, it turned into continuous internal strife. The dominant personality of Alexander put an end to this system, not by strength alone but by imparting a new and a better idea. He envisaged a kingdom under one ruler and he maintained that this system would ensure peace and progress. Many Greeks living in Mesopotamia, Egypt and Syria began to think of themselves as citizens of the world and were glad to be free from the restrictions and bondage of the city-state. It was not simply that they had changed their residence, they had changed their ideas. Their thinking was on a different plane and could no longer be limited by the petty rivalries of the old regime.

As a corollary of this there came new ideas of religion. The legendary hero-gods, the local deities and the unknown gods were no longer sufficient for a people who travelled the world. Had the local deity the power to help the soldier struggling in the Indian jungles? How did the old idea of the local god fit in with the concept of the great outside world? They heard the Jews talking of Yahweh and the Persians extolling the glory of Ahura-Mazdah, and these were regarded as supreme and powerful. Was it not time that the Greeks began to re-think their position in relation to their gods? And these questions led not only to a new world of ideas but to a new world of the spirit.

ALEXANDRIA

One of the ways of spreading these new ideas was by building cities which had a definite Greek flavour. There were many of these but the greatest was Alexandria. It was a model city. Spacious, clean, cosmopolitan, well planned, it remains as Alexander's greatest memorial. Situated on the shores of the Mediterranean it was a healthy city. Its irrigation was all the year round.

The canals were drained every summer but were soon filled again by the overflow of the Nile. Strong north winds swept away the silt of the Nile and gave the city an ideal harbour. The city had five sections named after the first five letters of the Greek alphabet, and the Jews lived in Delta. The streets were on a rectangular plan and some of them were thirty yards in width. The Palace with its Museum and magnificent library was on the sea front, and the light-house was one of the wonders of the world.

It was a centre of culture, and it is safe to say that few cities have had a greater influence on the thought of mankind. Travel had made a vast difference to the general outlook on education. The Greeks were to discover that other folk had original ideas too, and that their own ideas were all the better for being challenged by others. It was an age of enquiry, experiment and enlightenment, and because there was a thirst for knowledge, there were notable advances in many fields of thought, in philosophy, science, medicine, art and literature. In this process Socrates had done a great thing: he had taken philosophy to the man in the street. He had made men question themselves. His aim was to prompt questioning, and even if the suggested answers were sometimes complicated abstractions, they were genuine attempts at solutions. This new attitude to learning had a salutary effect on the scholars. Demand brought supply and it is no exaggeration to say that the epics of Homer, the poetry of Euripedes, and the prose of Plato, brought new horizons of hope as well as knowledge to people of every class.

The demand for knowledge brought the organization of knowledge. Schools, libraries and university centres gave an added impetus to the new outlook. Three new ideas which Hellenism brought to the world must now be stressed: the freedom of the individual, the necessity of education, and the ideal of universalism.

The first of these might be illustrated by an incident from the life of Alexander himself. He had gone to visit the famous Cynic Diogenes, and, standing before him where he sat in the open air, had asked if there was any boon he could confer on him. "Yes," he answered, "move from between me and the sun." The Greeks knew the Conqueror's saying, "If I were not Alexander I would be Diogenes," and the polite answer, "If I were not Diogenes I would be Alexander." And this is the point to notice: the Master of the World and the Rejector of the World met on an equality. This is individual freedom in its most explicit form. To find a humble beggar saying to a World Conqueror, "Move from between me and the sun" indicates a freedom of thought, speech and action, which has eluded many forms of later civilizations. Diogenes had found intellectual freedom; as he said, he "had never been a slave since Antisthenes set him free." He had no fear because there was nothing to take from him.

The necessity of education is seen in the various schools of Thought which arose in many parts of Alexander's Empire. Of course the combination of individual freedom and the passion for knowledge sometimes had queer results—follies, fanaticisms, and futile speculations—but the risk had to be taken. Alexandria was a bee-hive of movements, sects and philosophical schools, but it was from this centre of intellectual activity that the thought of the world was being re-shaped.

Previously there had been civic, national and religious exclusiveness everywhere. Judaism, carefully nursing the Ark, and jealously guarding the Law and Covenant, yet missing the true purpose of her mission to mankind, had already begun to show that ossified orthodoxy and rigid exclusiveness which have characterized her religion ever since. Although in another chapter we have been almost lyrical in our praise of the basic tenets of the Jewish Faith, we still must face the fact that it is this persistent exclusiveness, whether it is based on racial, national or religious grounds is beside the point, this exclusiveness has virtually turned Judaism into a noble sect when it was meant to be a dynamic Faith. So the new universalism of the Greeks, especially in its practical outworking, had something to teach the Jews.

The halcyon days of Egypt's greatness were long since past, but her decline was not due only to military defeat, for there was a deeper reason. Egyptian religion had been incurably nationalistic and by this time it had twindled into a series of esoteric beliefs which were passed on from one generation to another. There was no message here for the outside world. Of course the situation was changed by the coming of the Muslims in A.D. 661 and this released Egypt completely from her insular religion and the shackles of the past. Nevertheless, the work was half done when the city of Alexandria was built and Greek influence was felt in Egypt for the first time. So this spirit of universalism was a factor in the deliverance of Egypt also. Even though the idea of universal brotherhood was still no more than an abstract idea, it was an idea which clearly indicated a way forward in the life of man and in the progress of the race.

ALEXANDRIA AND THE CHRISTIAN RELIGION

It was necessary that someone should arise who could apply the specific methods of Greek philosophy to the new material supplied by the Christian religion. The Greeks were never easy to satisfy and it was necessary to present a reasoned theory about God and the universe. The facts of Christianity had to be so interpreted as to yield a concept of God which would at least conserve His unity and yet admit of His connection with man as Lord and Saviour. What was the importance of Alexandria in fulfilling this purpose?

As a result of the syncretism of the period together with a remarkable spirit of toleration, the atmosphere was congenial to Alexandrine Christian scholars like Clement and Origen. A mutual dependence of Christian and heathen was one of the most pronounced features of the age. The Christian philosophers knew that the Greeks would appreciate the allegorical method so they applied this to Christian thought. At the same time they stressed that all popular deities were really attempts to express the manifold activities of the one God. They did not overlook the fact, however, that all such expressions culminate in the life of the God-man, Christ Himself. Their primary task was to harmonize the Apostolic Tradition concerning Christ with the theological conclusions of the Jewish Alexandrine Philosophers. At the same time they had to protect the Church against too great a readiness to make concessions to the demands of philosophy. They succeeded in stating the case for Christianity in philosophic terms but they did not exchange the Gospel for Neo-Platonism.

In the sphere of theology Clement was a pioneer. It was he who first realized that Christianity must face the challenge of the secular philosophers of the age. But for his clear mind and cogent expositions the Christian Faith might have faded away into an esoteric cult. But Clement read the signs of the times correctly and saw the vital necessity of putting Greek philosophy in the service of the Christian Faith. His real distinction is that he opened the door of Christianity to the cultured Greek. He was always on the look out to further this cause and his liberal approach is evidenced by the fact that he welcomed people of any race or religion to his classes in Alexandria. Professor Hort said of him: "There is no one whose vision of what the faith was intended to do for mankind, was so full and so true."

Clement had three aims: to train all his pupils for Christian living, to show them that the secret of Christian living is in the possession of true knowledge, and to show that in the life of the ideal Christian true knowledge and perfect love are combined. It is fair to say that the ground had been partly prepared by some of the Greek Philosophers who lived about two hundred years before Clement. One of them was

Epictetus whose main concerns were: to speak on all occasions as if God were present, to remain at the post which God has assigned as one's first duty, and to make it the ultimate purpose of life to sing to God. Such men obviously prepared the way for the Christian interpretation of life.

To sum up it may be said that Alexandria became the intellectual battle-ground of the world. Four streams of thought contended in the struggle—syncretism, secular philosophy, Gnosticism and Christianity. The outcome of this struggle was threefold: firstly, it revealed that Christianity could withstand the intricate and penetrating scrutiny of Greek philosophy; secondly, that it was possible to use philosophy to give a more convincing interpretation of the Christian Faith, and thirdly, it banished forever the unreasonable prejudice that Christians were low, coarse and uncivilized. A religion which had drawn into its ranks men of the intellectual calibre of Clement and Origen, Justin and Athenagoras, could no longer be dismissed as nonsense. So perhaps Alexander's greatest victories were not won on the battlefield after all, but in providing those facilities in Alexandria which were instrumental in re-shaping the thought of the world.

CHAPTER XV

THE RISE AND INFLUENCE OF ROME

THE MONARCHY AND THE REPUBLIC

Rome had been in existence a thousand years before she could claim to be the greatest power in the world. Certainly her ascendancy had been slow but it had been thorough, and her influence was greater than that of any of her predecessors. By A.D. 200 Rome was the capital of an empire which virtually spanned the world. She then held a position of superiority which is unrivalled in the annals of history. She was acknowledged to be the Queen of land and sea. Although she had great rivals—Antioch, Jerusalem, Alexandria, and another which was soon to be her greatest rival, Constantinople, there is no doubt that Rome's place was supreme. Rome's position was due to Roman Law, Roman Government, and Rome's military strength. She had given her name to that ordered system of government and civilization which marked off imperial citizens from barbarians, and in the far-flung corners of empire men claimed with pardonable pride that they were citizens of Rome. For the origin of this mighty empire we must go back to the early settlers on the banks of the Tiber nearly a thousand years earlier. History and poetry join together in giving us the date of the beginnings of Rome.

> It was a calm and silent night,
> Seven hundred years and fifty-three,
> Had Rome been building up to might,
> And now was Queen of land and sea;
> No sound was heard of clashing wars;
> Peace brooded o'er the hushed domain:
> Apollo, Pallas, Jove and Mars,
> Held undisturbed their ancient reign,
> In the solemn midnight
> Centuries ago.

Although the second line is history as well as poetry, in lines five and six the wish seems father to the hope, for it cannot justly be said that the Romans ever reached the state when they abolished their expansionist policy and were content to rest on their laurels. But the theory behind lines five and six was commonly accepted. Dante was only

118

echoing the sentiments of Augustine when he declared that the Roman Empire was a cradle which God had prepared for the birth of His Son. He goes on to describe Constantine as founding the city in the East which was called by his name so that "he might give the Shepherd room." It is one thing to recognize and assess the value of Rome's achievement in preparing the way for the coming of the Christian Gospel, but it is quite a different thing to glamorize and romanticize those achievements so that Rome looks more like a tinselled fairyland rather than the hard, disciplined empire of a Roman Caesar. Nevertheless Rome had almost reached the Zenith of her power on that "clear and silent night," and certainly in the two hundred years that followed she attained a position unparalleled in the past.

In the days prior to the Republic (750–500 B.C.) there was social unrest. The Romans were soon to find that when they had thrown out the kings (509), mainly because they were of Etruscan stock, they had not solved all their problems, and certainly not the problem of power. The struggle between two distinct social classes continued, the patricians representing the aristocratic party and the plebeians representing the common people. The cause of this deep-seated division is not known but it is possible that Sabines and Etruscans who joined the earlier settlers on the banks of the Tiber, tried to lord it over the original settlers, and that the class distinction caused by this attitude was perpetuated.

When the last of the kings, Superbus, had been driven out, the plebs really got down to the task of claiming their rights. There were three important landmarks in the process:

(a) The plebs insisted on election to the magistrate body.

(b) The Twelve Tables were drawn up and the patricians could no longer capitalize on the ignorance of the plebs.

(c) In 367 B.C. the rule was established that one of the two consuls should be a pleb.

No sooner had these tough problems been sorted out in the final century of the Republic than a long conflict began between Rome and Carthage—the Punic Wars. The first was from 264–241, the second 218–202, and the third from 149–146. From all these Rome emerged successfully, although she suffered a serious defeat at the hands of Hannibal in the second Punic War (216). The defeat of Carthage made the Romans hungry for further victories and within a few years Macedonia and Syria were added to Rome's spoils. Meanwhile the situation in Italy itself worsened, the Social War taking place in 90 B.C. This was a struggle in which the people outside Rome demanded equal rights and equal citizenship with the people in Rome. The result was a compromise: the Romans asserted their authority but conceded the franchise to their compatriots to keep the peace. Ten years later the old class struggle revived, Sulla leading the Nobles and Marius the People. Terrible massacres took place in a Civil War which accomplished nothing. One of Sulla's generals, Pompey, emerged as a strong leader who, after campaigns in Cilicia and Syria, returned to Rome and joined forces with Julius Caesar and Crassus in the first Triumvirate. This joint arrangement was shortlived, and Caesar being the ablest of the three soon asserted his authority. Caesar's assassination increased the troubles and left the leadership question wide open once more. This time Octavian, Mark Anthony and Lepidus formed another Triumvirate which became another signal for war between the rivals. Lepidus was no more than a passenger and soon fell away. Octavian and Mark Anthony divided the empire between them and immediately began to quarrel over it. Octavian decided the issue by his victory at Actium (31 B.C.). He then became ruler of Rome, Head of the Empire and received the title 'Augustus.' Ten other Caesars followed but with the exception of Vespasian they were non-entities and are only remembered as tyrannical, bloodthirsty men. The four emperors who ruled between A.D. 96–180 were men of different calibre— Trajan, Hadrian, Antoninus and Aurelius—who did much to re-establish peace and prosperity in the empire. But the men who were chiefly responsible for the rise and influence of Rome were Julius Caesar and Augustus and we must now consider the nature and scope of their achievements.

THE EMPIRE

Julius Caesar 100–44 B.C. Caesar stood at one of the great turning points of history. He presided over the end of the Republic and the dawn of the Empire. Apart from dealing firmly with troubles at home, where he vanquished Pompey, he successfully conducted campaigns in Gaul and Spain. If clever strategy and opportunism won for him many military campaigns, his personal magnetism won him many a struggle on the political front. He did not easily win friends but he knew how to command obedience. Caesar was no sychophant; others had been carried to positions of power by appealing for the support and loyalty of the legionaries, Caesar imposed his own will on men and events, and did what others had not dared to do—he invested power in himself.

He bore all the marks of genius. His first master-stroke was to assume the leadership of the democratic party even though he belonged to the aristocrats. This clever ruse won the general support of both parties and from 58 B.C. till his death he was the supreme ruler of the empire.

He managed to convince his people that this new arrangement was for the good of Rome. Once this idea was firmly instilled into their minds he took to himself the three principal offices of state, those of home affairs, foreign affairs and the direction of war. He did this without any apparent constitutional upheaval. It was part of his statesmanship that he recognized that anyone holding these three key positions would be master of the empire.

But he had another advantage: he was the first to recognize that the days of the Republic were over and that the old pattern of the self-contained City-state was no longer workable. Caesar was an expansionist and was swift to realize that the greatness of Rome depended upon the greatness of her empire. If he drew wealth, materials, grain, craftsmen and technicians from the colonies, he was also keenly aware that Rome had much to give. It so happened that what she had to give was something which the colonies most needed. There was vast potential both in men and materials in North Africa, Spain, Gaul and Britain, and he believed that it could be developed only if it were brought under the direction of Rome. It was Caesar's achievement that he was able to exploit and develop these new resources to the full. But Rome's contribution was vital. Principles of government, sound laws, engineering, means of communication and education —these were Rome's gifts to her empire.

Caesar was a good democrat so long as he was in charge. Nevertheless, it must be admitted that it required a strong ruler to keep peace and order over so vast an area. In many respects he was a benevolent dictator and followed the good example of the Persian rulers in his merciful treatment of conquered enemies. Some of his associates doubted the wisdom of this course but were not strong enough to challenge it. He deluded the people more than once 'for the good of Rome,' and he was not above using any means that might achieve Caesar's ends. For instance, he introduced popular elections but it is not unjust to say that the vote was little more than Caesar's rubber stamp.

He held his power by the careful choice of provincial rulers and by his quite genuine concern for the welfare of the people at large. He threw open the Senate to representatives of all classes and even appointed freed slaves to high office in the colonies. His economic and agricultural reforms brought a higher standard of living for the poor and his granting of Roman citizenship to the colonies was perhaps the greatest civilizing agency that the western world had so far known. He provided a state library in Rome on the model of that in Alexandria, and some of the provinces soon followed the example. He reopened schools of Latin in Rome, and the study of grammar and rhetoric was given high priority. Along with the interest in education, he showed interest in recreation also and bequeathed the Emperor's gardens to the people. While it is true that all these innovations and reforms served to strengthen his position, they also served to provide an empire in which people were better fed, better educated and better ruled than at any time in the past.

From any standpoint Caesar's murder was a tragedy. He had the strength, vision and will to make Rome greater still. But a man who takes power unto himself and whose haughtiness, pride and self-will cause him to disregard the advice and aspirations of everyone else must always wear his crown insecurely. Caesar was murdered by men who found it impossible to break with the past and who could not face the changing pattern. The light of the City-state was lost in the glare of empire, and this was too much for them. Caesar himself typified this radical change, so their course was clear. But his assassins were like Lilliputians tripping on the mighty body of a Gulliver. The one thing that relieves the sense of tragedy is that Caesar was succeeded by a man of similar fibre, whose achievements were scarcely less spectacular and equally effective in the cause of empire. Caesar's was a work of conquest, it was left to Augustus to consolidate the gains.

Augustus (65 B.C.–A.D. 14). Augustus ruled more wisely and much longer than Julius Caesar. But these two great emperors had much in common. Both were practical men rather than intellectuals. The scholarly emperors—Trajan and Aurelius—were to come later. Again both Julius and Augustus believed that universal Roman dominion was a destiny determined by God, and both were bent on its fulfilment. Both believed that character was developed in the school of discipline and by undertaking vast and perilous enterprises. Both men held firmly the reins of power and both knew that the secret of governing an empire lay in the choice of rulers who represented them abroad. Generally they chose men of quality and loyalty, and although occasionally a procurator had to be recalled, that was the exception, and on the whole, Roman rulers in the colonies justified the trust placed in them. But they were greatly assisted by that twin instrument of Roman rule, Roman Law backed by the Roman Army. Both Julius and Augustus were concerned about preserving the pax Romana and both were empire builders. Julius kept the peace with a gaze from his 'falcon eye' and with a swift flourish of the sword, while the more eirenic methods of Augustus were more effective and more readily accepted. But Augustus was second to none in his determination to extend, strengthen and consolidate the empire. The Romans, not by nature a sea-faring nation in the sense of the Phoenicians and the Greeks, had the utmost respect for rivers both as a means of defence and of attack, and the legions were at the ready on the banks of the great rivers of the empire—on the Nile, the Rhine, the Tyne, the Danube and the Jordan. Augustus marked out the boundaries of the empire and it says much for the thoroughness of his work and the example of his rule that those boundaries were almost identical four hundred years later.

But in other ways the two men were very different. Julius was the type of man who could only look one way—ahead. His theme-song might have been: "Tomorrow to fresh woods and pastures new." Like the mariners of the sixteenth century he was out to discover and conquer islands and continents unknown. Augustus had more the attitude of Napoleon who took his men to the foot of the Great Pyramid and said: "Gentlemen, forty centuries look down on you." Augustus appealed to tradition and history, and found inspiration, Julius staked everything on the future, and found challenge in it. Julius was concerned to stress the stability of the family and the need for simple domestic religious ritual, Augustus restored old temples, built new shrines, punished wrong doers, encouraged dynamic thinkers, and in every way kept religion and conduct to the forefront. For Caesar religion was a formal affair and it was useful because it kept people's minds occupied. Augustus recognized that the whole of the social and political life of Rome depended upon her religion. He commanded the respect and obedience of his people but discouraged Emperor worship in Rome. As his power grew, his fame spread, and in spite of his wishes on this matter, Emperor worship became an accepted cult in many of the colonies. It was not a separate cult but was linked with Mithraism which, as we shall see in a later chapter, was the religion of the Roman soldier.

That Augustus was a soldier as well as a statesman is self-evident. He is famous for what may be called his two-edged policy. He was blessed with foresight as well as insight and he had a remarkable facility for solving two problems at the same time. For instance, after inflicting a heavy defeat on Anthony and Cleopatra at Actium in 31 B.C., he was quick to see that Egypt's grain would ensure a steady food supply for Rome. So at Actium he made his own position secure and discovered a granary as well. The same facility is seen in the way he dealt with fires. Fires were common in Rome where many houses were built of timber, and naked flame was used for light. He dealt with this problem not only by imposing fines for carelessness but by appointing fire-watchers to take night duty and by encouraging his people to build in stone. Another domestic problem was that of the idle and careless barbers of whom there were many in Rome. The razor slipped too often and not always accidentally. This he tackled by ordering the law to be read while the barbers were attending to their duties. This meant that they could no longer be idle, and the reminder of the penalty for carelessness had the desired effect. Further, divorces were common, and Augustus, invoking the Twelve Tables, insisted on the wife's right of appeal. He also insisted that in a divorce action a wife might reclaim her dowry and a maintenance allowance for their children. The Roman husband, often a tyrant in his own home, became much more prudent after these laws were enforced. Such examples might be multiplied but these are sufficient to reveal a man of high principles and resolute action who was keenly aware of the social problems of his day and of the means of their solution. All in all, Rome was fortunate in producing such a man to be her ruler and guide in the early days of the empire. Rome owed a great deal to Augustus, and the saying that 'he found it of brick and left it of marble' is true of Roman character as well as Roman buildings.

ROMAN LAW

Roman Law was part of the Roman ethos and was applied with typical Roman thoroughness. It is regarded as Rome's greatest contribution to western civilization. It is worthwhile noting:

(a) That the application of Roman Law was the secret of the greatness of the empire.

(b) That Roman Law was the direct result of the Roman genius for fusing the intellectual and the practical. It is doubtful whether it could have emerged in quite the same way in any other land.

(c) That Roman Law has been the controlling and guiding factor in the development of the western world.

How did it begin? In 451 B.C. ten decemvirs were appointed to draw up laws, and they drew up ten 'Tables' that year and added two more Tables in the following year. It is sometimes said that ideas were borrowed from Greece and especially from the legislation of Solon, but there is scant evidence for this assumption, and in any case the Twelve Tables are practical, clear and robust laws which are not likely to have emanated from Greece. While there may be uncertainty as to how far Rome was dependent upon Greece in matters of religion, philosophy and culture in general, there can be little doubt that her laws are essentially and distinctively Roman. There are two views about the origin of the Twelve Tables. The first is that they represent customary law, i.e. a legalizing of long accepted usages and customs. It must be realized that man held very tenaciously to the usages of the past, and eventually such a religious sanctity surrounded these ancient customs that they were assumed to have had a divine origin. The other view is that the Twelve Tables represented existing laws which were codified and systematized to fit the needs of the Republic. The first view does not exclude the second and the truth may lie in a combination of both.

There were public laws which related mainly to matters of public administration—the constitution of the state, matters relating to colonial rule, and the organization of public power. Private laws, on the other hand, referred to questions of individual relationships between citizens, and dealt with injury, debt, death, divorce, slavery and many other matters. The vital point to notice about the Twelve Tables is that they successfully incorporated the wisdom and jurisprudence of the past, brought stability to the state, consolidated the empire, and brought emancipation to Roman family life.

How did it develop? Early Roman Law developed in three stages: Interpretation by jurisconsults; Equity by the Praetor; and Legislation. The first stage consisted in the interpretation of existing law, the explanation of its contents as well as its adaptation to changing circumstances. The Praetor had the power to supplement, develop and even amend the law. Legislation meant the direct and open change of the law on account of its unfitness. Under the Empire this third method superseded the other two modes. It is interesting to note that customary law, Equity and Legislation have appeared in that order in English law.

ROMAN ROADS

With the exception of Roman Law nothing played so important a part in the growing influence of Rome as her system of communications. There was much coming and going in the early days of the empire and the Romans knew that good government was possible only if the colonies were directly linked with Rome. Where possible the Romans preferred to travel on solid roads rather than on the mercurial sea. Indeed they regarded sailing as a necessary evil. The roads were needed and greatly used. Trade routes to many parts of the empire were opened up; war captives and slaves were transferred to Rome; students travelled to other countries in search of renowned teachers, and armies were constantly transported to various parts of the empire.

Mr. Hilaire Belloc writes: "Swiftness and certitude of aim and a sort of eager determination which we are slow to connect with government, but which certainly underlay the triumph of this people." This really sums it up: the Romans knew what they wanted to do, did it and made the utmost use of it. Roman roads were built on high ground, and they were straight, direct and solid. Some of them in the Lake District are built across mountain ranges and can still be traced.

Great viaducts were built across valleys in order to link the road between mountains. Directness was everything, and time lost in building bridges and viaducts was later reclaimed because of the directness of the route. The main roads were connected so that in case of trouble troops could be sent speedily along the highway. It is impossible to overestimate the importance of these roads in the efficient administration of the empire.

ROME'S CONTRIBUTION TO CIVILIZATION

The title of this chapter "The Rise and Influence of Rome" was deliberately chosen because so often the emphasis has been on her decline and fall. Of course every nation must at some time decline and fall, but not every nation rises to such glorious heights or exerts so great an influence as did Rome. It is a pity that the writers of the early empire were cynical, critical and rebellious. Perhaps they were too close to events to give an impartial opinion, but at all events, their opinions virtually wrecked the reputation of Rome. The historians, knowing more about the halcyon days of the Republic, looked back with nostalgia and could see no good in the present. The poets who praised the regime, Virgil and Horace were accused of being in the pay of the emperor and this is probably true. The Stoics were not interested in worldly success, and perhaps were too blind to see anything good even where it was to be found. On the whole it may be said that Rome had a bad press and has never been able to live it down. In every age there are rebels, nonconformists, social misfits and angry young men. In Rome they had their say and their day, which is a pity because they have given a distorted picture of the facts. This is not to minimize or condone the low morals, love of power, cruelty, selfishness, intrigues and conspiracies which often marred the life of civic Rome. The empire eventually went the way of all flesh but it cannot be doubted that the influence of Rome remains. The greatest tribute to Rome is the continuance of the institutions which she founded and the endurance and stability which her law and government have brought to the civilized world.

The theory that at the beginning of the Christian era the world had sunk to the nadir of iniquity and was on the point of disintegration is very wide of the mark. The phrase 'the fullness of time' did not mean that matters could not be worse but that the opportune moment had arrived. The world was not on the brink of ruin, on the contrary, there was a general mood of wistfulness and men were looking up in hope.

The Hebrews had kept alive the belief in a supreme God who was Creator, Sustainer and Ruler of all things and who had promised to send a Prince of Peace to bring love, joy and peace to all nations. The Greek philosophers had set men thinking about the great problems of life and death and destiny, and even if their answers were tentative, they had at least created a climate of thought in which the fuller answers might be understood. The Romans had traversed the world introducing law and order and civilized methods of government. After all, times had been far worse than they were in the reign of Augustus. Pompey had cleared the Mediterranean of pirates, Caesar had largely succeeded in abolishing brigandage on the high-roads, Augustus was doing all in his power to conciliate the Jews and had shown understanding and sympathy to non-Roman slaves. All this does not present a picture of darkness and decline. It is rather an exciting introduction to a still more gripping story. The world was not waiting for the nemesis of disaster but for the dawning of hope. What followed was truly remarkable but it were foolish lightly to dismiss the massive labours of the preceding centuries. Rome's part in that time of preparation was considerable and perhaps there is much to be said for Dante's view that the peace of the early empire was God's way of preparing the world for the advent of his Son.

What the world really needed was a religion charged with spiritual power. Law, Philosophy and Rhetoric were all very well but they did not bridge the gap between belief and conduct. The beguiling ceremonies of the mystery religions evaded the real issue. The teachings of the Stoics, Epicureans, and Cynics did not satisfy the immortal longings that stir the minds of men in every age. The enlightened moralism of Greece had no answer to the problem of evil in man. Plutarch states the problem without any hint of an answer: "Mankind is always struggling from the rule of evil to the higher rule of God." The vital question is: is there any way in which this struggle can be resolved? Christianity deals with this the greatest of all issues. It affirms that God Himself takes action in His world, that a Redeemer brings the certainty of salvation to all mankind, and that the knowledge and experience which follow from this event transform every situation. Mankind is cursed by the love of power, Christ changes this concept by an assertion of the power of love. But if this power is to be effective, it must be operative in human life. It is the spirit of love in man which holds the promise of a new world. It was this love which transformed all relationships as the early Christians knew, which gave men courage in the face of death, and which sent men to the uttermost parts of the world with a message that could not be suppressed. This was not simply a new message, it was a new experience and it changed the lives as well as the thoughts of men of all races. If the world was waiting for the supreme event which was to make all this possible, who will dare to say that the years of preparation were in vain?

PART III

CHAPTER XVI

THE RELIGION OF EGYPT

THE KEY TO EGYPT

Egypt did not choose isolation, geographical factors made it a necessity. With a great expanse of desert on one side, mountains on another, and the Great Sea to the north, Egypt was cut off from the rest of the world. It is interesting to note that a great civilization was developing in Mesopotamia, quite independently of what was taking place in Egypt. The material needs of the Egyptians were assured by the annual overflow of the Nile and this gave them plenty of time to think and to pursue their own rather insular way of life. If the Nile became a fetish, it was because the lives of the people were so much bound up with it. It was one of the causes, if not the principal one, of Egyptian survival and prosperity. Irrigation, crops, food, drink, transport—all were dependent upon the Nile. Since the river was the main water supply, it acted like a magnet and drew people to it, so that towns and villages were built on its banks. In any case, no permanent settlement was possible out in the open desert. This great waterway was a necessity for their trade as well. No wonder Herodotus said: "Egypt is the gift of the Nile." Although it brought economic stability to Egypt, it also brought a pronounced conservatism to Egypt's religion and social customs. Secure from outside interference, at least till the beginning of the New Kingdom (1560 B.C.), she concentrated on developing her own institutions which, while very remarkable, had little influence on the outside world. It is not suggested that the Egyptians were inactive from the beginning of the Old Kingdom (3000 B.C.) and during the Middle Kingdom (2040-1730), on the contrary she made many significant strides in the spheres of engineering, building, and agriculture, but until the days of the New Kingdom their achievements and methods were unknown outside Egypt.

From the point of view of religion, until 1500 B.C., their influence beyond the bounds of Egypt was almost nil. Jehovah revealed Himself in the Sinai desert not to the Egyptians but to the Hebrews. Yet it should be added that towards the close of the Middle Kingdom, a young Pharaoh arose, Akhenaten, who had high hopes of introducing a new religion. His aim was to lead his people away from the worship of mythological gods to one supreme God. It is now generally believed that he did this for political reasons. In the first place, a universal God would be recognized outside Egypt, and in the second place, he himself being identified with Aten 'the Great God' would be worshipped by his subject peoples and this would strengthen his grip over them. Be that as it may, it was a significant development in a land of innumerable gods. The hymn to Aten is full of noble thoughts:

Thou risest beautifully in the horizon of heaven,
Oh living Aten who creates Life!
When thou risest in the eastern horizon
Thou fillest every land with thy beauty.
Thou art beautiful, great, gleaming and high over every land.
Thou art afar off, yet thy rays are on the earth;
Thou art in the faces of men, yet thy ways are not known.

This is sometimes dismissed as sun worship, but it should be remembered that the object of worship is not simply the sun's disk but its life-creating power. But perhaps this prophet came too soon, for his noble ideas perished with him and the old gods held sway. It should be noticed, however, that while Aten is thought of as the creator-god, nothing is said of his character or of his relationship with men.

'HOUSES OF ETERNITY'

Why were the Egyptians interested in embalming their dead? They stumbled across the fact that their soil and climate possessed remarkable preserving qualities. Even without any embalming process, in Egypt's natural conditions, bodies were preserved for many years. It was this fact which no doubt interested and surprised the Egyptians. When a corpse was specially embalmed it remained life-like for centuries.

Egyptians reasoned that bodies remained life-like because the spirit in them had survived. Could there be the one without the other? It was a short step to the view that if it were possible to preserve the body in this real and life-like fashion, it would also be possible to ensure the preservation of the soul. The two were thought to go together. They therefore gave careful attention to the embalming of the body, not for the body's sake, but for the sake of the 'ka' (spirit) within it.

But if the dead were to last forever and if soul and body were to be preserved, they should be given a suitable, even an elaborate abode. The more important the person, the more magnificent the tomb, and for the Pharaohs, a Pyramid Tomb. An Egyptian tomb was known as a 'House of Eternity.' It was built as such, and their boast that a Pyramid Tomb would last indefinitely was not a vain one. The purpose of the tomb was to do honour to the soul and protect the body from the effects of time; to prevent violation by robbers, and to furnish the spirit of the dead with such material needs—food and drink—as were thought to be necessary to ensure survival. Earthly houses might perish with time, the Houses of Eternity would not.

It should not be thought that the Egyptians were obsessed with the idea of death. They looked upon the tomb as a suitable guarantee of the continuance of life. They could think of no greater bliss than the perpetuation in the next world of the joys they had known in this.

The presence of two tombs for an individual has presented a problem. The custom is strange only to others, not to the Egyptians. It must be remembered that Osiris was said to have been buried in several places after his mutilation by Seth. Many Pharaohs had a tomb in Abydos, a holy place of great antiquity, and another in their capital, Memphis. It is probable that the Pharaohs themselves requested a tomb in the land of their fathers, near the holy shrine. If their tomb was near to the shrine of the God-king, it would be easier for them to enter the sphere of the blessed spirits. On the other hand, their subjects would demand yet another tomb in the capital city. Hence there arose the custom of building two tombs.

ADVANCED RELIGION IN ANCIENT TIMES

Long before the Egyptians and Hebrews met, there is evidence of ideals of social justice and humane conduct. For instance, the following inscriptions on the Pyramids of Gizeh give a clear indication of the moral sentiments of the people who wrote them:

> *Established is the man whose standard is righteousness,*
> *Who walketh according to its way.*
> *Although misfortune may carry away wealth . . .*
> *The power of righteousness is that it endures.*
> *Speak the truth, do the truth,*
> *For it is great, it is mighty, it is enduring.*

Those who have been greatly impressed by the man of endurance and moral ideals as portrayed in Job (written 400 B.C.), will be interested to see the portrayal of a good man found on an Egyptian tomb-chapel in 2000 B.C.

"There was no citizen's daughter whom I misused, there was no widow whom I afflicted, there was no peasant whom I evicted, no herdman whom I expelled. There was none wretched in my community, there was none hungry in my time. I did not exalt the great man above the small man in anything that I gave."

That the Egyptians attributed great powers to the sun god, Re, is indicated by the following verses from the Coffin Texts:

"I have made the four winds that every man might breathe thereof like his brother during his time."

"I have made the great waters that the pauper like the lord might have use of them."

"I have made every man like his brother, and I have forbidden that they do evil, but it was their hearts which undid that which I had said."

It is passages such as the above which have prompted some scholars to say that Egyptian influence upon the Hebrews was considerable. But this is not the only evidence. If Akhenaton was the Pharaoh who was conquering Syria and Palestine during the time that the Hebrews were under his rule in Egypt, it is reasonable to suppose that his ideas on monotheism would be communicated to others.

Further it is interesting to read the following in the Egyptian Book of the Dead:

"I did not slay men. . . . I did not steal. . . . My heart devoured not . . . (i.e. coveted not), I did not speak lies. . . . I did not commit adultery." This means that the sins forbidden in half of the Ten Commandments were also sins forbidden in Egypt when Moses was a young man. The first, as the record in Exodus makes clear, Moses was not likely to forget. We assume, therefore, that the mind of Moses had been prepared during the days in Egypt for the revelation which came to him in the desert of Sinai.

Such then is the story of the Ancient Egyptians' search for the good life. The astonishing thing is that when we first encounter them (3200 B.C.) they are already enjoying a highly developed civilization. In so many respects they were an advanced people: in the use of copper and bronze, in their architecture, carpentry, metal-work, jewellery, and in many other ways. The drive behind some of these magnificant achievements must surely have been something more than the legendary stories of Egypt's mythological gods. Nevertheless, it was the Osirian legends which utterly captivated the imagination of the Egyptian people, and perhaps the reason is that in those legends there is life and hope, resilience and resurrection, and a god who was near enough to be understood.

But before turning to a consideration of the Osirian legends, we must at least name some of the popular gods of Egypt. Ptah was the creator, always swathed in bandages because he belonged to the long past; Maat was the goddess of Truth who was in attendance in the Osirian judgment scenes; Safekht was the goddess of writing, and Anubis, the jackal guardian of the cemetery. The people were, of course, enthusiastic polytheists, for they worshipped not only the gods of Egypt but many which were imported from Babylonia and Persia.

THE LEGENDS OF OSIRIS

We come now to the favourite of all Egyptian concepts—the stories of Osiris. The main aspects of Osiris are as follows:

As a mythological god. These stories begin with Re, the sun. He produced Shu, the air, and Tefnut, the moisture or world-order. This was the primeval pair who in turn brought forth Geb, the earth, and Nut, the sky. From these two came two males—Osiris and Seth, and two females—Isis and Nephthys. Isis became the wife of Osiris and Nephthys, the wife of Seth.

As a human king. Alongside the above divine lineage there is also a human one. Osiris was said to be a great king who ruled over Egypt and taught the arts of civilization to his subjects. As a New Kingdom hymn says: "He established justice throughout both banks of the Nile. . . . Earth saw how excellent he was and entrusted the kingship to him to lead the two Lands into prosperity." In typical Oriental hyperbole it ends:

> His crown clove the sky
> And he consorted with the stars.

The reign of Osiris was regarded as the golden age and became a model for subsequent generations. The Egyptians believed that there had been a time of perfection at the beginning of the world, and just because Osiris was the cause of this perfection, he was looked upon as the source of perfection in all the ages that followed.

The conflict. It is at this point that the mythological elements and the idea of an earthly king become confused, and we have to accept the fact that in Egyptian minds the two concepts were interwoven.

The idyllic order under the rule of Osiris was destroyed by Seth, his younger brother. Seth tempted Osiris to lie in a chest, and having got him safely in it, Seth and his confederates threw the chest into the Nile. It is wrong to look for the location of this event; the important thing to remember is that wherever the rites were performed, Osiris was overcome and killed by his wicked brother. Eventually, the chest was washed in the flood and lodged in a tree. The tree was felled by the king of Byblos who used it to form the main column of his palace. In some way Isis knew that the body of Osiris was hidden in the tree trunk. She begged for the column, extracted the body of Osiris and took it back to Egypt. As a fertility god Osiris is sometimes regarded as a tree or as living within one.

All the sources agree that Seth tore up Osiris's body and scattered the pieces. Some say the fragments are all over Egypt, while others say they are in the Nile. But someone was seeking Osiris, someone who would not let him leave the world, it was Isis. She collected all the pieces together and brought them to one place, thus making the first essential mummy.

Isis revived Osiris and bore him a son, Horus. During this time Isis lived in the swamps of the Delta. Horus grew up and attacked the usurper Seth, and overwhelmed him. Although the stories are not easy to piece together and interpret, there are certain features which occur in all the legends.

Characteristics of the Osirian Legends. (*a*) There is the vital link with the Nile. Osiris is thrown into the Nile, he rises from it, and Isis lives in the Delta during the birth of Horus. Here again the Nile seems to be connected with the principle of resurrection.

(*b*) The curious thing is that Osiris is always portrayed as helpless and rather pathetic; he is always the under-dog, the one who suffers. Nevertheless he is resilient and is never utterly vanquished.

(*c*) He is never portrayed as strong and vigorous like the heroic gods of Greece, he is a swathed figure carrying the two emblems of Egyptian royalty, the crook and the flail. For while he is the life-spirit of earth and vegetation, he is also a mummy. He became the god of the dead and the judge of souls.

(*d*) Yet Osiris always typifies the spirit of the Egyptian past, and the fact that he survived in their thinking long after the Olympian gods of Greece had been discarded shows how strangely fascinated the Egyptians were by the Osirian legends. Many attempts have been made to group the Egyptian gods in some sort of neatly worked out system; it is a vain task because these stories are so diffuse and varied that they cannot be classified. Egyptian religion is like a store-house of bits and pieces of ancient stories and legends which have been sentimentalized and treasured for so long that no one has the heart or the courage to throw them away.

Osiris and the After Life. One thing is certain, Osiris is never left very long, either in the underworld or beneath the First Cataract of the Nile; the Pharaohs become the incarnation of Osiris, so it may be said that he becomes the power and inspiration behind the most absolute monarchy the world has ever known. Yet it was not Osiris as incarnate in the Pharaoh who was most feared, it was the Osiris who presided in the after life.

One of the chapters in the Book of the Dead is on the Negative Confession, and this is clearly an attempt to introduce something like an ethical system into Egyptian religion. The first part deals with sins against the gods, and the second part catalogues the sins against the

King and men. Faults of character are emphasized: lying, greed, sudden anger, vanity and arrogance. Whether people observed them or not they still had to submit to trial before Osiris, so they were never allowed to forget him.

Heaven is the kingdom of Osiris. No one seemed to know the location of the Osirian Fields; were they in the Delta, or far away beyond the Syrian Sea, or perhaps in the Milky Way? At any rate it was a pleasant place where there was an abundance of grain, plenty of shade, and endless happiness. The procedure was this: the soul was brought into the Hall of Truth by the Jackal-headed god Anubis, and placed before the enthroned Osiris who was attended by Isis and Nephthys. The soul would begin to justify itself not by a confession of sin but by telling the evils it had *not* done. Then the dead man's heart would be balanced by Anubis in the judgment scales against an ostrich feather. If it were a heart made light by goodness, it was allowed to pass to the blessed Osirian Fields, but if the scales proved the soul to be evil, then retribution overtook it. Perhaps there is a link with the Hebrews here also, for what the Egyptians pictured the sky goddess as doing when she raised up the departed, so a Hebrew might have pictured Yahweh doing: "She sets on high again for thee thy head, she gathers for thee thy bones, she unites for thee thy members, she brings for thee thy heart into thy body." It is this ineradicable principle of resurrection which gives the Osirian legends a perennial appeal.

CHAPTER XVII

THE RELIGION OF PERSIA

ZOROASTER AND THE BUDDHA

Zoroaster (660 B.C.) was born in Persia about a hundred years before the Buddha was born in India. Both were great leaders and thinkers and each became the founder of a great religion. Although living in different countries both were born into communities where the Vedic gods were worshipped, and both opposed idolatry. Both men offered different solutions to the problem of Vedic polytheism. Nature deities and man-made images were virtually irrelevant to the Buddha's main purpose, while Zoroaster discovered a God (Ahura Mazda) who transcended them all. Both were founders of religions, Buddhism and Zoroastrianism, which have survived to the present day, though neither is closely connected with the country of its origin. The birth of each man was accompanied by miraculous events and each man received a definite divine call. The first became a philosopher-mystic, the second a moralist prophet.

While the Buddha was born into a royal family, Zoroaster belonged to a farming community. While the Buddha proposed to his people one aim—self-renunciation, Zoroaster proposed to his people one God—Ahura Mazda. Buddhism was slowly squeezed out of India by the persistent pressure of disgruntled Brahmins, but Zoroastrianism was driven out of Persia by the sword of Allah. The Buddha offered deliverance through self-realization, Zoroaster offered deliverance through the decisive conquest over evil—the victory of Ahura over Ahriman. No one knows what might have happened if the early Buddhist missionaries, the emissaries of the great Buddhist King Asoka, had turned West as well as East, but as it is, Buddhism has been mostly confined to the continent of Asia. On the other hand, if the Zoroastrian King, Xerxes, had not been defeated at Salamis (480 B.C.), the Faith of Zoroaster might have entered Greece and become one of the major religions of the western world.

THE VEDIC RELIGION

The link, however, between Persia and India does not begin with the advent of Zoroaster and the Buddha. We have to look further back in order to discover why both men had a similar religious background. In the dawn of history the great Aryan people split up to form the leading nations of Europe and Asia. What was the religion of the Aryans before they were divided? They honoured a vast number of gods who governed some distinct aspect of life. All their gods were connected with nature; they worshipped the sky, the sun, the moon, the dawn, the wind, and fire.

After the division one portion of the Aryan family took up its abode in Iran, the other moved into territory on both sides of the upper Indus. This people, ancestors of the Zoroastrians and creators of Hinduism, maybe designated Indo-Iranian. The Vedas are the scriptures of the Hindus and the Avesta is the literature produced by Zoroaster and his followers. It is from these two sources that we learn something of the religion of these two groups. The Vedic gods are in three groups:

The Gods of the Earth: Agni, Soma and Yama.

The gods of the Air: Indra, Vayu and Rudra.

The gods of the Heavens: Savitar, Vishnu and Varuna.

Among the Persians Agni, the god of sacrificial fire, became more and more important, while among the Hindus, Varuna, the all-seeing god and judge of all, and Vishnu, the preserver of life, who assumes many incarnations to fulfil his purpose, gained prominence. A noble verse in the Rigveda shows us how they tried to understand the meaning of the powers in the universe:

They call him Indra, Mitra, Varuna, Agni; and he is the heavenly noble-winged Garutman.

To what is one sages give many a title: they call it Agni, Yama, Matarisvan.

Garutman means the Sun and Matarisvan the Wind. Such was the nature worship which prevailed in Persia when Zoroaster came on the scene.

A NEW PROPHET ARISES

It has already been stated that Zoroaster was born in 660 B.C. and although this date is now accepted by many scholars, there are some who place him a century earlier. The suggestion that he belongs to 6000 B.C. must surely be regarded as a printer's error! The circumstances surrounding his birth were remarkable. It is said that the glory of God "came down from the endless light and mingled with the mother of Zoroaster." When he was born his face shone with a divine light, and instead of crying as most infants do, he laughed outright. This was supposed to be the first sign of his later career as the prophet of victory, but this idea is probably due to the enthusiasm of his devotees. We notice in those days the beginnings of Astrology, and if like all Persian boys Zoroaster was attracted by the lights of heaven, he also showed a strange interest in the lights of earth, and spent many hours experimenting with light and fire. It is said that in a little cave in the hills he used to wrestle with the great problems of the solar system, and fire and light helped him to understand. Whether these experiments have anything to do with the emphasis on fire worship in Zoroastrianism we do not know, but the connection cannot easily be dismissed. Apart from this strange fascination, he had a normal boyhood, receiving the sacred thread (kusti) at the age of fifteen as a sign that he had taken his religious vows. Although there was a practical realism about his cave experiments, he was a sensitive boy and felt keenly the sufferings of others. His compassionate nature was revealed by his care for people and cattle during times of famine. At twenty years of age he left home in search of an answer to the religious questions which troubled him. He sought enlightenment anywhere and from anyone. He was so serious in his search that he always hoped the next person he met would be able to provide the answers that he sought. It is said that he spent seven years meditating in a cave, waiting for the moment of truth. The idea that he was in the wilderness for twenty years and lived only on cheese is a later invention but it makes a good 'commercial.' At the age of thirty, a crucial age in the life of Jesus and the Buddha also, the moment of enlightenment came. He was standing on the banks of the Daityu River when he was confronted by a divine messenger. This messenger was Yohu Manah (Good Thought) who told him to mount in spirit to the Celestial Assembly where he would meet Ahura Mazda, the Wise Lord. There he received his prophetic call and was given his message. He was so utterly overawed by the presence of Ahura Mazda that all the little Vedic gods seemed like candles under a searchlight. He had now met "the Great God who had created heaven, earth, mankind." He had seen God as Holy, as Light and Fire, and he was bidden appeal to him to know the Right. He was told that he had one duty—to obey. "Speed thou, ere my angel of judgment come, followed by treasure-laden Destiny who shall render to men severally the destinies of the twofold award."

With deep conviction and with a joyful heart he set out on his mission, but like many other prophets he was soon shocked by the blatant hostility to his message. His own sense of elation made it even more difficult to believe that others did not wish to listen to him.

His failure to win disciples greatly troubled him though he never questioned the reality of his vision. The hostility of others was a severe test of his patience, and an aggressiveness crept into his message. In fact, in the early days of his mission a more reasonable approach would have brought more promising results. His message became tinged with arrogance as when he maintained that he alone had been set aside by Ahura for a great task and counted all others who claimed this divine prerogative as men of falsehood. "I was ordained at the first by thee; all others I look upon with a spirit of hatred." Also there were times when he brought pressure to bear upon those who refused his message. For instance, he advised Prince Vishtaspa not to pay tribute to Prince Arjasp because the latter refused to accept the new Faith. Perhaps on occasions his religious fervour clouded his judgment, but on the whole, he faced his task with courage and hope despite all the disappointments.

Yet these set-backs were preparing him for his future message, even though he was unconscious of it. He regarded his failure and sense of frustration and despair as brought about by *temptation*. The idea was not new but the emphasis upon it was quite extraordinary. Evil was not a theory to be argued about but a battle to be fought. Ahriman (Angra Mainyu) was not simply a vague principle at large in the universe, he was thought of, perhaps for the first time, in personal terms. This doctrine gave a new edge to the power of evil and a new urgency to the plans and actions of Ahura. In his temptations Zoroaster was repeatedly asked by Ahriman (The Lie, the Bad Spirit), to renounce Ahura Mazda, and each time he made the brave reply: "No I shall not renounce the good Religion of the worshippers of Mazda, not though life, limb and soul should part asunder."

After ten years of preaching, his own cousin became his first convert, but the real break through was the conversion of Prince Vishtaspa. His conversion was complete and lasting and he used all his powers to propagate his new Faith. He led several campaigns against enemies of the Faith one of which was against the fearsome Turanians. If it is argued that the path of the Faith should not be made by the sword, the answer is that there is more excuse for this in 600 B.C. than for the Muslims in A.D. 600 or the Christians in A.D. 1600.

THE PLEDGE

The Zoroastrian Pledge is as follows: "I repudiate the Daevas. I confess myself a worshipper of Mazda, a Zarathustrian, as an enemy of the Daevas, a prophet of the Lord, praising and worshipping the Immortal Holy Ones. To the Wise Lord I promise all good; to him, the good, beneficient, righteous, glorious venerable, I vow all the best; to him from whom is the cow, the law, the (celestial) luminaries, with whose luminaries blessedness is conjoined. I choose the holy, good Armaiti (Piety), she shall be mine. I abjure theft and cattle stealing, plundering and devastating the villages of Mazda worshippers."

But Zoroastrianism was not merely a matter of words; the pledge was intended to prompt right action. Zoroaster was no doctrinaire, and he defends his dogmatic attitudes on practical grounds. Good and evil are not clearly defined in the way the Hebrew prophets defined them, nevertheless Zoroaster points to the practical difference between them. Goodness means to accept the true religion, evil means to reject it. Goodness is to oppose the daevas (demons), evil is to submit to them. Goodness is to speak the truth and help the followers of Good Thought, Evil is to submit to the Lie (Ahriman) and help the bad. Goodness means to till the soil, raise the grain, grow fruit, root out weeds, reclaim waste land, irrigate barren land, and to treat animals kindly, the evil do not concern themselves with agriculture and that is their downfall. Those who do not seek the practical good of all are out of harmony with Mazda. They are in harmony with Mazda if they remember and apply the four great virtues of man: liberality, justice, friendliness and sincerity. These virtues are applied when the three great duties on man are observed, and these are:

(*a*) To make him who is an enemy, a friend.
(*b*) To make him who is wicked, righteous.
(*c*) To make him who is ignorant, learned.

THE TEACHING

Zoraster's most significant contribution to religious thought is the consistency of his teaching on the supremacy of Ahura Mazda. Mazda was the Lord, and this paramount fact solved many problems. He was impatient of any denial of this truth and he was sure that ultimately Light would defeat all the powers of darkness and Mazda would be seen to be supreme.

Mazda was the Lord of Light, the Father of Right, and the Lord of Wisdom. It is true that he was opposed, but it was an unequal struggle and the supremacy of Mazda was never in doubt.

Zoroaster's confidence in this truth is revealed in his attitude to the daevas. The daevas were the Vedic gods, and in the relentless logic of his system they could not retain their original status. They were not abolished but superseded. Although in Hindu thought they have retained their original importance (all Hindu gods are called devas), in Zoroastrianism they have been relegated not only to a minor role but to a different one. They have become no more than symbols of the evil forces of nature and the name daevas has come to mean demons.

They were still active in the universe but were seen for what they were—forces arrayed against the supremacy of Mazda.

Zoroaster managed to avoid a difficult theological problem by introducing two new insights: first, that evil forces were brought into being not by Mazda but by Ahriman; and second, that while they were strong enough to withstand everything else, they could not withstand fire. The dualism, therefore, is modified because evil powers were always under the threat of destruction, a fate which could not even be considered in relation to Mazda.

Having put the daevas in their place, so to speak, Zoroaster then turned to another opposing party—the Magians. The theory, commonly held, that the Magians were Zoroastrians is incorrect. The Magians (Magi) were magicians who believed that by consulting the stars and repeating magical formulae they could drive away evil spirits, heal diseases and control natural forces. The truth is that Prince Vishtaspa marched against the marauding nomads of the north (the Karpans and the Turanians) precisely because they had succumbed to Magian beliefs and practices. With their numerous animal sacrifices, their magical procedures, and their control of demonic influences, they were in direct opposition to the teaching of Zoroaster. It is true that the Magians eventually became a strong Persian hierarchy, but the Zoroastrians were least true to their founder when they adopted such beliefs.

THE SACRED FIRE

The followers of Zoroaster are sometimes deridingly called fire-worshippers. The phrase is unfortunate partly because it savours of idolatry and partly because it is a caricature of the true Faith. Whatever weaknesses there may be in Zoroastrian beliefs, idolatry is not one of them. We have seen that the symbols of Fire and Light have played a prominent part in the development of this religion and the reason is that these symbols represent the holiness of Mazda, for the name means 'Light.' A Zoroastrian writer puts the matter in true perspective: "Think not that our fathers were worshippers of the fire itself: they fixed their eyes on the splendour of the exalted flame while they humbled their spirits before God."

There are other reasons why the Sacred Fire is important in their teaching. They had a passion for purity. The reason why modern Zoroastrians, the Parsis, place their dead on the Towers of Silence is because a corpse would defile the earth. It is not, therefore, buried in the earth but placed on the stone floor so that the elements may remain pure. But apart from this, the virtue of purity is extolled in the Avesta:

"Purity is for man, next to life, the greatest good . . . The religion of Mazda cleanses the faithful from every evil thought, word and deed, as a swift-rushing mighty wind cleanses the plain."

Another reason why the Fire symbol is prominent is because Zoroaster is said to have carried a 'cube of fire'—a kind of porous, luminous substance which represented his gospel of Light. According to tradition he was done to death while serving before the Sacred Fire. In the Gathas he says: "At every offering of thy Fire, I will think me of Right so long as I have power." He was thinking of Right in his last moments, and when Zoroastrians remember the Fire they remember Mazda and his prophet.

A further reason for the perpetuation of the Fire symbol is this: at the end of time the final test between good and evil will be an Ordeal by Fire. Ahriman and all the powers of evil will be overcome and the Light and Fire of Mazda will emerge triumphant.

It remains only to be said that some of the great Persian rulers—Cyrus, Darius and Xerxes found inspiration in this Faith, and their well-known generous and humanitarian attitude to their conquered enemies is a striking testimony to the influence of their Zoroastrian background. Alas! when the Sassanid rulers of Persia were conquered by the invading Muslims in A.D. 651 they were not treated so generously. Those who remained in Persia were compelled to accept the Faith of Islam, while those who fled to India carried their Faith with them. This small but energetic and forward-looking community still upholds Mazda's Fire and Light which no human conqueror has managed to put out.

CHAPTER XVIII

THE BUDDHA AND BUDDHISM

A NEW GURU (560–483 B.C.)

Only India could have produced the Buddha; China might adopt him but she could not have produced him. Burma might welcome him, but she could not have nurtured him. Yet he has greater honour and allegiance outside India than within it. He has become the patron saint and object of worship for many people in eastern lands, yet India has few Buddhist shrines. The reasons for this must wait.

But the reason why the Buddha essentially belongs to India and could not have emerged anywhere else is because he was the child of the advaita doctrine of classical Hinduism and this was unknown outside India at least until the time of Alexander the Great. Another reason is that only an Indian versed in Advaita doctrine could have given such a radical interpretation of its philosophy. And this is another way of saying that the Buddha is in the true tradition of the Indian mystic or rishi or sannyasi or sadhu, except that in the range of his influence and the depth of his thought he surpasses them all.

It is significant as well as interesting to notice that all the great founders of religion have appeared in the eastern hemisphere—Zoroaster and the Buddha, Moses and Muhammad, to mention only some of them. In fact, all these come from the Middle East as does Jesus of Nazareth. If we include the teaching of the Sufis as the finest expression of Islamic mysticism, we may say that all these outstanding religious leaders brought to the world a similar message. They all stressed that religion was a way of the most rigorous self-renunciation and of detachment from the world. With the exception of early Islam, they are distinctly other-worldly in emphasis. The teaching of Jesus, as against those events of His life which are determinative for a true understanding of Christianity, has much in common with other leaders especially on spiritual detachment and union with God. The purpose of Our Lord's training, struggle and temptation is twofold: to achieve purification of soul and to find perfect union with God. Jesus said: "It is the Spirit that quickeneth, the flesh profiteth nothing." Again he said, "He that loseth his life shall find it." and in the Sermon on the Mount we read: "Blessed are the pure in heart, for they shall see God." All the same, it must not be forgotten that the plainest statement Jesus makes on this subject proves that he is not thinking of personal purification but of the purification of others: "For their sakes I sanctify myself." It is hard to find this particular motive in the teaching of the Buddha. Personal purification, it seems, takes precedence over everything else.

There is no doubt that the Hindus and the Buddhists look upon Jesus as one who sought perfect union with God. They often quote the 'Vine' passage where Jesus taught that his followers maybe as closely united to him as the branches to the vine. Their own Scriptures say: "He who knows the Life of life, the Mind of mind, the Self of self, in him there is no diversity." As far as they are concerned salvation consists in overcoming separateness. They believe that Jesus had reached the summit of spiritual experience and fulfilment when he said: "I and the Father are one." After all, the Upanishads had already said: "He who truly knows the supreme Brahman becomes Brahman." Nevertheless it is necessary to add that Jesus was seeking something more than perfect union with God. The Christian Faith holds that he had that already, but he sought something else.

These great leaders had one thing in common: they presented to the world a new teaching, won many devotees and became founders of new religions. The accepted custom in eastern lands whereby a religious teacher wanders from place to place spreading his message was undoubtedly a great asset to all of them. A climate which permits outdoor meetings at any time and place was always a great help to a Guru seeking to win new disciples. But perhaps there are two deeper reasons for their success: the first is that the East remained for many years untouched by the industrial revolutions of the Western World, and was for the most part immune from the materialism which followed from them. And secondly, there is a profound respect, even reverence, in eastern lands for the man who renounces the world and its evil ways, and seeks the life of detachment, meditation and prayer. Such a man will never be short of food and shelter, and if he is genuine, he will not be short of followers either.

A PRINCE AT HOME

Few men have won the reverence and admiration of the people of eastern lands as successfully as Siddhattha Gotama. Gotama was born in 560 B.C. in a small kingdom named Paderia in Southern Nepal. His father, Suddhodana, belonged to the warrior caste, which is a curious circumstance when Gotama's message is borne in mind. His mother, Maya, died when Gotama was seven days old and he was brought up by his mother's sister who also was married to Suddhodana. Strange things happened at his birth and these were regarded as signs that he had been appointed as 'the Enlightened One.' When he was born he was received into a golden net which was held by four angels who handed him to Maya with great rejoicing. Immediately he received the offerings of gods and men and joined in the song of victory which began: "The chief am I in all the world." The Brahmins who were present foretold that he would become either "a universal monarch," or, if he retired from the world, a Buddha. His father, a rajah himself, was greatly disturbed by these strange signs, and while he did not appear to mind his son becoming a universal monarch, he was unreasonably perturbed at the thought of his son retiring from the world. He became unusually possessive, and resolved to protect his son from the evils and sufferings of the world. He reasoned that while a man may flee from the evil in the world, he is not likely to flee from a life of wealth, luxury and pleasure. But this was the father's idea, it was certainly not Gotama's. The father, no doubt, sensed this and consulted a wise man: "What will my son see to make him retire from the world?" The answer was that the turning-point would come when Gotama saw a decrepit man, a man full of disease, a dead man, and a devotee. This answer was sufficient to make Suddhodana determined to prevent his son seeing any of these. When Gotama was sixteen his father built for him three palaces and provided everything for his son's satisfaction and happiness. Gotama was not impressed. He was a studious and reflective individual, and the opulence and splendour of palace life left him cold. He never felt at home in it. He seemed always to be thinking of something beyond the palace walls, and he felt driven into the outside world by some inward power. During the period of waiting, despite all his father's efforts to divert him, he spent much of his time doing good, acquiring knowledge, practising asceticism and seeking Nirvana.

EMANCIPATION

In spite of all the precautions, the day came when Gotama saw the four dread omens: an old grey-headed toothless man, a man foul with disease, an uncovered corpse being carried to the burial-ground, and a yellow-robed ascetic with a calm and peaceful face. His father had been proved right at least in this: that the sight of these figures would shake his son's life to its foundations. Gotama was now possessed of a horror of life. He became obsessed with the idea that life was no more than a ceaseless round of rebirth, sickness, old age and death. The greatest evil was life itself and there must be some way of escape from it. This problem he had to face; how did he face it?

At the age of twenty-nine, now married and the father of a son, he could hold out no longer, and left home to find solitude and a quiet refuge in the jungle. The immediate cause of the break was the birth of his son. He had enough ties already that were holding him back, and he soon realized that this would be the greatest tie of all unless he took action at once. He sat cross-legged under a Bo tree, having reached the nadir of dejection. Just when all hope seemed lost, light came. The mystery was made clear, his mission was clarified and his message revealed. The suddenness of the experience surprised him, but the reality of it was beyond doubt. From now on he was the Buddha—the Enlightened One. Having spent four weeks in fasting and meditation, he rose up and went under a banyan tree nearby where he sat for seven days enjoying the sheer bliss of emancipation.

A NEW MESSAGE

He was now a man with a message. Previously he had had no wish to proclaim anything. But he had waited until he was sure. Brahma had commanded him and under this new compulsive power he had no option but to obey. The question haunted him: How can I best serve my people? He must divulge his secret for he believed it was the secret of existence; he must proclaim to everyone the way to emancipation. He began with three universals: all life is transitory, all life is misery, and all life is illusory. This may not appear to be a very promising note on which to start a new philosophy, but if it is doleful it has about it the ring of reality. When human life is carefully examined, it must be confessed that there is much in it that lacks permanence, happiness and reality. This may not be a popular message but it was the Buddha's conception of realism. He was not particularly concerned about how his doctrine sounded, he was concerned about the truth. However, it may not be as pessimistic as it sounds, and perhaps there are philosophies which are more hopeful but less realistic. All the same, we should understand the Buddha better if he sometimes offered a faint ray of hope instead of the gloom and finality of death. Of course it is true that in this mortal life, change is inevitable, but is there never a transition to something better? So often he begins with promise but ends in despair.

> While life is good to give, I give, and go
> To seek deliverance in the unknown light,
>   Unto this I came,
> And not for thrones: the kingdom that I crave
> Is more than many realms—and all things pass
> To change and death.

Generally speaking the change that takes place is a change to a deeper misery. It is rather like a man standing in quicksands, the more he struggles to get out, the more he sinks in. The Buddha never equated truth and suffering but the trend of his teaching came very near to it. It was necessary to believe that life was misery so that it might be overcome. But sometimes he seems to speak in riddles—only misery is unaware of being miserable. Only the abstract is real, never the personal. The underlying reality is the way, not the man who seeks it.

> Misery alone doth exist none miserable,
> No doer is there; naught but the deed is found,
> Nirvana is, but not the man who seeks it,
> The Path exists, but not the traveller on it.

On the positive side Buddhism does enable man to look at life fairly and squarely, unfettered by emotional tensions and personal prejudices, and to this extent its teaching is helpful. Also there is the constant reminder that reality exists and may be discovered. It is hidden by one layer after another, but when these are removed, Reality is disclosed. Change, sorrow, ignorance and illusion must be removed if emancipation is to be attained. The certainty of emancipation need not be questioned, for it rests on the evidence of the Buddha's own experience.

The trouble is that there are many things which appear to be real which are merely illusory, and this applies to life itself. This brings us to two of the Buddha's original contributions to Indian thought, contributions which were revolutionary in their consequences though uttered by the least revolutionary of men. It was these ideas which brought about a complete break with Hinduism, the Faith in which he had been brought up. The Buddha never put forward a world view because he was not greatly interested in this world. He never envisaged a perfect social order because the social order itself was unreal. The caste system was part of the social order. This theory, therefore, undermined the caste system which was part of the very structure of Hinduism. On this showing the whole caste system is a massive illusion and need not be taken seriously. It is unthinkable that any orthodox Brahmin would take this point for it would mean that his prestige and authority would vanish in a night.

But if the Buddha undermined the caste system, he also took the sting out of Karma—the doctrine that life itself is the result of past deeds, whether good or bad. If there is no real soul to be reborn, rebirth can be brought to an end. If this happens, the idea of Karma as understood by Hinduism, falls to the ground. Such a doctrine could not possibly thrive alongside Hinduism, and perhaps this is the reason why Buddhism has almost disappeared in India while gaining ground in countries which have no historical back-log of caste and Karma. For the Buddha, Karma is the 'law of becoming' but it has no link whatever with transmigration. In Buddhism there is no living soul to connect each life with the next or to act as the dwelling-place or agent of Karma.

THE FOUR NOBLE TRUTHS

The first Noble Truth is that suffering is inescapable. In his own day the Buddha would have little difficulty in convincing his hearers of this particular truth. He could not forget the reason which first drove him from his palatial retreat. Birth, illness, decay, death—all involved suffering. He could not get away from the fact that all things seemed doomed to decay. To see this happening was to experience the most intense suffering. The absence of things we love is suffering; the presence of things we hate is suffering; not to attain Nirvana is suffering, and therefore life itself is suffering. What the Buddha feared was not death but life, for it was life that involved endless suffering. Time after time he asked himself the question: "How shall I in this world of suffering, be delivered from suffering?" Yet he welcomed suffering as a means of attaining the good life.

He had to ask a deeper question: what is the cause of suffering? The answer to this was the Second Noble Truth—the cause of suffering is desire. It is the desire for existence, for pleasure and for prosperity. The Buddha did not define this condition as sin, but if sin is defined as self-centredness, then the Buddha would no doubt have accepted it. The four prohibitions laid down for his followers are concerned with this Second Noble Truth.

(a) An ordained monk may not have sexual intercourse.

(b) He may not take what has not been given him—not even a blade of grass.

(c) He may not knowingly deprive any creature of life.

(d) He may not boast any superhuman perfection.

The Third Noble Truth follows from this: the path to the cessation of suffering is the destruction of desire. Psychologically the question arises as to whether any human instinct can ever be destroyed. On this showing we have to die to know Nirvana. Of course man's baser instincts must be controlled and mastered but this is a different thing from their extinction. But the Buddha set great store by the powers of trancelike concentration, and obviously believed that it was possible to bring instincts and desires under the complete control of the mind and spirit. He was no mere theorist but a practical teacher of ethics.

He gave the people simple rules of conduct and, beginning with these, exhorted them to aspire to Nirvana. The second stage was renunciation—the going forth from 'Home' to 'Homelessness,' and here again the Buddha was himself the pattern of his precepts. They were bidden to strive and strive,

> Till every throb of lust is rooted out,
> Expunged is all the fever of desire,
> Cool am I now and calm—Nibhana's peace.

The last step was the attainment of wisdom when the knowledge of the non-ego and the impermanence of all things are personally realized. This involves the strenuous efforts of concentration but it is the only way to deliverance:

> Blest is the lesson my teacher hath taught,
> I live in the village but ever in thought
> I escape to the jungle: no fetters for me,
> For wisdom hath made me most gloriously free.

Deliverance is not possible by knowledge, asceticism or action of any kind, it is possible only by INACTION—that is the great secret of Buddhist philosophy. But the destruction of desire is a negative doctrine; does the Fourth Noble Truth suggest a more positive approach?

How does a man attain this "Exceeding store of joy and of impassioned quietude?" The answer is simple: he must follow the Eightfold Path. This shows that Buddhist teaching is not entirely otherworldly, otherwise the Buddha would not have realized the immense practical value of this Path. The Path is made up of various qualities; there are three groups. The virtue group: true speech, right action, and an honest vocation. The concentration group: the right use of the memory, continuous aspiration, and the rapture of meditation. The knowledge group: true beliefs and true attitudes.

The logic of these Four Noble Truths should be noted: Here is fact, and this is the cause of it. Here is the cure, and this is the way to find it. If this is a true statement of his message, what has happened to his mission?

AN EXAMINATION OF BUDDHIST TEACHING

The question is often asked whether Buddhism is an atheistic system. It is difficult to give a straight answer to such a question because part of the strength of Buddhism is that it is non-committal on so many important truths. It is as if the Buddha is saying, "I tell you what I know, and I am not prepared to say more." The Buddha nowhere defines what he means by the character of the Absolute. But to refuse to give a definition does not necessarily mean to deny the existence of the Divine Being. Buddhism is somewhere between a religion and an ethical system. If religion means a relationship with God, then Buddhism is less than a religion. On the other hand, it is more than an ethical system because while it is concerned with outward conduct it also lays great emphasis upon an experience of inward peace. Perhaps it is best to call it a mystical philosophy of life. It is primarily concerned with this life. In Buddhist teaching the question of the Future Life seems to have nothing to do with the fact of deliverance. If this life is set in a minor key and if it is not worth living, there can be no true longing for a Future Life. On this matter also the Buddha was non-committal, yet it is fair to say that many modern Buddhists believe that they have acquired sufficient merit to ensure them of a happier existence after death. But there is a serious limitation even in the Buddhist interpretation of this life. It is true that there is the aim of personal emancipation but there is no goal for mankind as a whole. The experience put forward is exclusively personal and the hope of a better world seems almost an irrelevance.

We are bound to draw the conclusion that the Buddha's work is more therapeutic than curative. He brings to sick men a revelation of the *symptom* of their disease, but mankind persistently cries out for something more. Moreover, the conception of the highest good as "the state of complete painlessness" in open to question. The goal of inaction is no goal at all.

Yet modern Buddhists rightly feel that they can offer to the world a way of peace, and it is precisely such a way which the Western World has failed to give. It is based on an inner attitude and assurance, and to those who find it, the experience is real and lasting. Since this experience demands the right kind of temperament and an advanced method of contemplation, it excludes too many who are just as needy but have little hope of attaining the experience they desire. But this is not to underrate the validity of the experience to those who find it.

The Buddha named no successor nor did he leave any detailed instructions as to how his movement should be organized in the future. This may have been due to his cynical attitude to the world and to any human organization, but that Buddhism has suffered by this neglect is beyond compute. This is one of the reasons why the movement did not fulfil its early promise in India. Another reason is the repudiation of caste which the Hindus could not tolerate. This was a brave and praiseworthy stand to take—the only step towards social reform in the whole movement. It is sad to say that this progressive step completely jeopardized Buddhist progress in India. But the main draw-back has been the way in which Buddhism has clung to the thought-forms and customs of the sixth century B.C. and her inability to apply her message to current needs. However, in recent years a new dynamism has entered into the Buddhist religion, and decisive steps have been taken to educate and evangelize in many lands, and this being the case, the future seems bright with hope.

CHAPTER XIX

SOCRATES (469–399 B.C.)
AND PLATO (429–347 B.C.)

SOCRATES

The Greek Mind. A modern cultured Greek carries with him the secret of his forbears. It is impossible to converse with him without recognizing this secret. The Greeks are masters of argument, of the incisive phrase and penetrating insight, and their range of knowledge is quite phenomenal. For instance, a priest will take a four-year course in Law so that his mind will be the better equipped to understand and present Christian truth. The Greeks are indisputably the greatest controversialists of all time. They press their questions hard and relentlessly as if all of them have been trained in the Socratic school. They are not yet troubled by television in Greece so a budding Socrates can still have a fair fling. If it is remarked to a modern Greek that it seems strange that Socrates left no written record, the reply will be prompt and final: neither did Jesus, neither did Gotama; why should it seem strange? There is one word which he will use more than any other, it is the word 'why,' so it will be seen that the Greeks have not changed very much. A member of the Greek Orthodox Church will say: "It is a great thing to be a Greek but it is a greater thing to be a Christian;" thus in one sentence he places nationalism in its true context in relation to religion. And although he is proud of the past glory of Greece and of the wisdom of her ancient philosophers, he is ready to concede that they lived before the deepest truth was disclosed to men. It is strange to find that the Greeks, even with their great love of tradition, think that our great national churches are more like museums than places of worship. "Do you emphasize the dead ones or the Living One?" It is precisely this facility for asking the crucial question and seizing upon the vital point that has given the sharp edge to Greek thought throughout the centuries.

It will be the greatest of all tragedies if, through outside political pressures or internal reactionary forces, the fire of Greek dialectic is quenched or the verve of Greek discussion subdued. The world will never be so rich in thought that she can afford to spare the insight and vision and vitality of the Greek mind.

The Sophists who prepared the way for Socrates represented much that was good in Greek Thought but they spread their net too wide. This meant that their haul was indiscriminate and they needed someone with a selective and analytical mind to sort it out. Also, their sights were too low. "Man is the measure of things," Protagoras had said, but Socrates could not leave this statement unchallenged. What is the authority for making such a statement? Who is to say what is the true measure? What things are referred to—animate, inanimate, divine? All these and many other questions must be asked. Indeed in the mind of Socrates the simplest proposition raised innumerable questions but rather than ask them, he was content to do the prompting, leaving others to do the asking. As the process of cross-examination went on, he pressed hard and long until the answer that was sought was elicited from the mind of the questioner. If the Sophists' net was too wide and their sights too low, their judgments also were too severe. "There is no truth," they said. But this sort of cynicism is the end of everything. If there is no truth, why trouble to seek? If there is no truth, what is the meaning of life and where are the standards of thought? If there is no truth, by what right does a Sophist affirm that there is only falsehood? Nevertheless the Sophists achieved something: they made discussion fashionable, philosophy popular, and a liberal education the greatest aim in life.

Removal of Prejudice. As has already been said, Socrates never wrote a book, nor did he introduce a new system of logic, nor did he become the founder of a school of thought. He was an explorer in the realm of knowledge. He saw himself as a guide leading the way through a jungle of ideas. He was first in the line, and on the way he lopped off branches to the right and to the left, he trampled down the undergrowth, and used every faculty of his being to do one thing: to make a way. By this method he was able to remove difficulties and to open up a new world of reality. There were so many difficulties to be removed —depression, pessimism, prejudice, tradition, and false assumptions. Socrates wanted to substitute reason for prejudice. Many of our judgments are based on prejudice and it is strange how they persist. There are prejudices, for instance, about the Jew and the Negro. Some years ago an American research worker gave some school children the following silent reading test: "Aladdin was the son of a poor tailor. He lived in Peking, the capital city of China. He was always lazy and liked to play better than to work. What kind of boy was he: Indian, Negro, Chinese, French or Dutch?" To his bewilderment, most of them said the boy must have been a Negro! But how do such prejudices arise? What causes them and what is the cure? Such was the task of Socrates, he wanted to remove the unreasoned and the unreasonable prejudice.

Another hindrance was the power of tradition. This was a drag on men's actions as well as their intellectual development. It is implied in the expression: "We have always done this and we have always accepted it without question." This was the gravamen of Socrates' charge against the men of Athens, they had accepted so much without question. But it does not require a man to say: "We have always done this," a monkey can live and move by that philosophy. Tradition must always be re-examined and must never be accepted without question.

Socrates maintained that people were living on false assumptions. They were not willing to remove falsehoods and face new sets of facts. He wanted to sting them into action. So, in addition to likening himself to a guide in the jungle, he also likened himself to a gadfly stinging the noble Athenian horse to awaken her from her lethargy and get her on the move.

Yet he knew that there was a price to pay, for the pioneer is never free from criticism and perhaps condemnation. Indeed it is conceivable that Plato had Socrates in mind when he told the story of the shipwrecked mariners. The mariners were perplexed and angry because one of their number suddenly began to take his bearings from the stars. They had never known anything like this before and were persuaded that their fellow-mariner had gone mad. They therefore lashed him to the mast and sailed on—on to shipwreck. They had incapacitated the only men who knew the true course and who could lead them to the harbour. Perhaps it is true to say that, in the end Socrates himself was brought down by those very false assumptions and unreasoned prejudices which he sought to remove. But this does not mean that he failed.

The Tribunal of the Mind. Socrates was concerned with the question: What is man? Archaeologists sometimes find evidence of six different civilizations on one site. They can demonstrate how one temple has been built upon another in different ages. Eventually they reach the rock bottom floor of the first temple built on that site. Socrates wanted men to get down to the rock bottom floor of their understanding. He thought the Sophists were concerned about too many things—astrology, cosmology and metaphysics, but he wanted specialization and he chose his theme: the mind of man. Perhaps he was the first real psychologist as well as the first philosopher.

Everything had to be brought to the tribunal of the mind. The minds of men are often bogged down by generalizations, exaggerations, customs and pragmatisms, which are not based on truth. So by conversation and cross-examination Socrates set out to reveal human ignorance. Unfortunately many thought that they were wise. His first task was to persuade them to ask the right questions. So his message runs something like this: virtue is knowledge, vice is ignorance, and deliverance from ignorance is salvation. He spread this message everywhere. He reckoned that given sufficient time he could elicit the right answers from illiterate slave boys. And it is certainly true that in every walk of life he met people, conversed with them and enlightened them. It was not so much that he put new ideas into their minds as that he made them analyse their own thoughts and apply them to everyday life. He also impressed upon them that the acquisition of knowledge was life's greatest pleasure. The epitome of his message was "Know thyself" or more properly "Know thine own ignorance." Sometimes his concept has been criticized. Coleridge is referring to Socrates when he writes:

> *Know thyself, and is this the prime*
> *And heaven sprung adage of the olden time !*
> *Say, canst thou make thyself? learn first that trade;*
> *Haply thou mayest know what thyself had made.*
> *What hast thou, man, that thou dar'st call thine own?*
> *What is there in thee, man, that can be known?*
> *Dark fluxion all unfixable by thought,*
> *A phantom dim of past and future wrought,*
> *Vain sister of the worm—life, death, soul, clod,*
> *Ignore thyself, and strive to know thy God.*

The criticism is not as forceful as it sounds. Socrates was, in fact, emphasizing his own ignorance. When he was pleading his cause before the Delphic Oracle, he said, that although he knew nothing else, he knew one thing, his own ignorance. He also knew that others who had not made this discovery thought themselves wise. But this was because they were not willing to examine their own minds. "An unexamined life," he said, "is not worth living."

He was one of those rare souls who live ahead of their times, and the men of Athens did not like his ironical approach. He seemed to make sport of many of the things which they treasured. In the end three accusations were levelled against him: that he did not believe in the gods of Athens; that he had introduced other divinities, and that he had corrupted the minds of the youth of Athens by his new doctrines. Certainly he had a strong dislike for the mythological tales about crimes among the gods, and to that extent he was guilty of discarding the traditional gods, but they had a hard task in proving the other two charges, if indeed they ever succeeded. But whatever the defects of his doctrine were said to be, there is no doubt that his teaching and his character were tested at his trial. His doctrine upheld him, giving him patience and serenity, and in his last hours his character shone forth in great splendour. There is a noble utterance at the end: "Now it is time we were going, I to die and you to live; but which of us has the happier prospect is unknown to anyone but God." So the quest and the questioning persisted to the end, and perhaps the secret of his calmness was that he had reached the stage when he was able to attribute all knowledge to God.

PLATO

In Search of Reality. "Plato," as Emerson said, "is Philosophy; he consumed his own times and absorbed the learning of his own times." By doing this he placed men of all ages in his debt. Plato was in search of Reality. He did not begin with assumptions about the world and draw from them conclusions about the Good. Hindu Vedanta philosophy begins with three great assertions: that man's real nature is divine; that the aim of life is the realization of this divine nature; and that all religions are essentially in agreement about this aim. Plato is more cautious about man's real nature, for he has first to discover Reality in the hope that all other things will fall into their proper place.

To the question: Is Reality to be found in the human senses? his predecessors had replied in the affirmative Their approach was "Beauty is in the eye of the beholder," which is to say that a thing exists because it is seen to exist. Any passing appearance is real in the moment that it is perceived. Plato was not content with such a theory because it vested Reality only in the human senses and denied existence to things that were not perceived. Plato taught that Reality existed independently of the senses. Even when an object cannot be seen or heard or touched, it is still real.

Aristotle begins with the concept of change, and concerns himself with the causes of this state of flux. Plato rejects the idea that Reality is confined to temporal things and looks for unchanging being. The Good which is the True and the Real shines everlastingly like the sun in the heavens. Man, dwelling in the cave of his ignorance, and bound by the chains of selfishness and strife, takes the shadows on the farthest wall for realities. Only when his eyes are cleared will he see the Real. The wise man turns away from the world of sense and keeps his inward and spiritual eye directed to the world of eternal ideas. Plato does not deny that temporal things contain partial truths but these derive their meaning and rationality from unchanging being.

Aristotle sets out to prove that there is a Cause behind all temporal things; Plato accepts the fact that unchanging Reality exists and then attempts to explain its nature. Aristotle is concerned with causes, Plato with values. But Aristotle finds Reality in the 'here and now,' while Plato finds Reality beyond the temporal world.

In Plato's teaching 'Reality' and 'the Good' are names for God. God is the cause of all good things and of nothing else because he is of a beneficient nature. God is supreme and does not change because change would be detrimental to him. Plato had to choose between the active side of the divine nature with its emphasis on the mind, and the passive side with its emphasis on the emotions. If he had accepted the latter, God would have been subject to passions and desires like human beings, but God was greater than that and could not be subject to human emotions. We have seen that the Olympian Gods—Zeus, Jupiter, Cronos and the rest were often in conflict with one another. They were continuously involved in emotional tensions. Their feasts and orgies, their loves and hatreds, their deception and vindictiveness, were well known to the Greeks, and part of their popularity was due to their 'human' traits. Platonic doctrine left no room for gods of this sort, and it is certain that Plato sounded the death-knell of the Olympians. But it was not simply that he disapproved of gods who were subject to human emotions, he had no room at all for Homer's polytheism. His doctrine of one unchanging being left the Olympians superfluous.

The Soul is immortal and imperishable, and Plato bases this doctrine on its divine origin. Since God cannot wish to destroy his own work and since nothing else can destroy it, the soul which is made by God in his own image, cannot be destroyed. The truth behind the parable of the cave is this: the soul once lived in a world of ideas but fell into a world of senses and was imprisoned there; but the memory of the good, the true and the beautiful remained and induced the soul to yearn for the world of ideas. By reverencing these ideas even while dwelling in the world of the senses, the soul is raised higher and higher until it reaches its true destiny. This doctrine of immortality results in an optimistic attitude to life. In this respect Plato's attitude is very different from that of many Greek writers who are unfailingly pessimistic. Plato forbids grievous lamentations at death on the grounds that a pessimistic attitude towards death is incompatible with belief in immortality. The soul which experiences purity and temperance has God for its companion and guide, and ultimately dwells in the place which befits it. But the soul that is impure or stained with evil has no companion or guide and lives in extreme distress until it is borne away to another habitation. Socrates obviously thought that he had deserved such a companion and guide for he prays that his journey to the gods might be prosperous. Both Socrates and Plato regarded death as a release from the fitful fever of life.

According to Plato, every soul, like mercury, finds its own level, and this idea leads him to the doctrine of Rebirth. It is found in the parable of Er at the end of the Republic. Yet his idea of reincarnation is different from that of the Hindus in one important respect. The soul's welfare in another existence is not determined by indifferent gods or by some ineluctable law but by the soul itself. The soul is not involved in an arbitrary cycle of rebirths, it possesses the power to choose. The great question is whether a man in his next incarnation shall be good or bad. The answer is given that whatever happens in the next life will be entirely due to the soul's own choice. Salvation to the Hindu is to escape from rebirth; for Plato, it is to be filled with Reality.

But this does not mean that the soul is free from judgment. To the young man who denies God's government of the world by a life of continuous transgression, Plato says: "You shall assuredly never be passed over by God's judgment, not though you make yourself never so small, and hide in the bowels of the earth, or exalt yourself to heaven: you must pay the penalty due, either while you are still with us, or after your departure hence, in the house of Hades, or it may be, by removal to some still more desolate region."

Emphasis is placed upon what a man believes. Plato tells of an absolutely just man who yet passes for an unjust one, and suffers the most severe penalties with no hope of release in this life and no expectation of reward in the next. When Socrates asked if such a soul could be happy, the answer is given in the affirmative because the man did not look at life simply from an earthly point of view, but believed in the spirit of man and in the significance of the universe.

The Guardians. These are the philosopher-rulers who govern the affairs of the city. Indeed in Plato's thinking only philosophers are qualified to rule. Plato appeared at the end of the Golden Age of Pericles in Athens, and was no doubt grief-stricken by the calamities which had befallen the city. The section on the Guardians hints at some of the reasons for the decline of Athens. The art of governing is to do the best thing for those who are governed. The Guardians must be both spirited and gentle, like a dog that is friendly with acquaintances but antagonistic towards the unacquainted. Earthly happiness must not be the intended end, for too much wealth and pleasure brings incompetence and inability. Temperance is the hall-mark of a well-governed state. People should not live in idle opulence nor yet in dire poverty. Women should be allowed to assist in government if they possess extraordinary gifts. New projects should be undertaken continually so that everyone may be employed. Interdependance was stressed, and each worked for the good of others as well as for himself. All the citizens should be fearless, and therefore no fables should be told to the children if those fables had false implications. Truth resulted in courage, falsehood ended in fear. One of the ways to end fear was through education. There was also a deeper reason: all citizens must be educated because knowledge was virtue.

Justice is the key-word in relation to conduct. Each one is expected to fulfil his vocation with temperance, bravery and wisdom. Although Plato emphasized these qualities he appeared to think that they applied only to a select few and that the poorer classes had no hope of reaching them. This notion had two defects: it was defeatist and it introduced class distinctions. Temperance meant that a man was satisfied with his lot. His duty was to accept and not to argue about it. The trouble with Greek thinking is that virtue is commensurate with a man's intellectual grasp, and this means that the poor and ignorant man has little hope of attaining the Good.

Plato comes very near to India's caste distinctions when he argues that every man must keep his appointed place. Men's abilities varied, and those who were inferior were fit only for manual labour, and those who were intellectually superior should have positions of responsibility. But even Plato was being inconsistent here for he was not allowing for the results of education. Fatalism might be defensible, but education had the power to change the situation. But this attempt to place people into neat categories will not do. The following words are familiar:

> The rich man in his castle,
> The poor man at his gate,
> God made them high and lowly,
> And ordered their estate.

And this, no doubt, sounded a very useful jingle in the ears of the eighteenth century slave-owning baron, but it had a hollow ring for the slave-driven labourer. These notions, like Plato's ideas on this subject, sound strange to us and indicate an odd idea of justice. But the eighteenth century was influenced by Calvin's teaching that the social system should be let well alone since the whole thing had been determined by an immutable decree; and justice in Plato is something less than a moral ideal, it is really a method of governing the city.

In order to govern adequately, reason must be supreme. When passion compels a man to silence the voice of reason, the soul becomes angry with itself because of its weakness. Anger is the result of passion overcoming reason, and it is the purpose of reason to keep under control the passions of the soul. Whatever dethrones reason and enthrones passion is worthy of blame. The Homeric poems aroused in men passions that were unworthy of reason, and that is why Plato condemned them.

The Value of Platonic Teaching. How shall we assess the value of Plato's philosophy? He himself maintains that there are three types of works: the works of God, the works of the man who truly creates, and the works of the man who imitates. Although he does not apply these to his own work, it is fair to say that it includes all of them. It contains inspiration, creative art, and analogy. His aim is to discover what is good. This discovery is made by gradual stages. There is a story in the Gospels about a man who was blind, who later was able to see men as trees walking, and ultimately was able to see clearly. Plato takes us along the same path in his doctrine of 'becoming'. Man is blind through his own ignorance, but later he is able to sort out the realities from the shadows, and eventually he is able to see Reality clearly. Or, as Plato puts it, first he sees only shadows, then he sees the original objects of which the shadows are a reflection, then he sees the sun which is the cause of all.

Why is the Republic still studied? It is outstanding in its aim. It is not merely a treatise portraying a perfect state, it is rather a eulogy of those virtues which make possible a perfect state. It is outstanding also in its comprehensiveness, touching on many great themes. It deals with the idea of God, the soul, immortality, with human virtues, moral ideals and spiritual realities. And it does this, not in isolation from the ordinary life of man but in direct relation to it. If his head is sometimes in the clouds, his feet are firmly on the ground. It deals with basic principles and not with dated situations. Its greatest achievement is that it successfully relates the practical to the ideal and sets the whole drama of human life on a divine and cosmic stage.

The crucial question arises: can such a dream ever be realized? Can anything be as perfect as it is described in the Republic? The question may be answered by permitting Plato to ask his perennial question: what is good for man? It is good for man that such a dream should exist. It is good for man that his mind should be stretched to comprehend such a dream. It is good for man that the process of 'becoming' should create an awareness of unchanging being.

It is true that sometimes the shadows are stressed overmuch; it is true that the sort of existence Plato envisages seems reserved for a few prophetic souls; it is true that a God who is implacable and immutable can neither love nor suffer; it is true that the doctrine of the Last Things in Plato is that there is no last thing, and that the dreary cycle of events continues indefinitely; it is also true that the barriers which prevent the soul from attaining Reality are not clearly defined; nevertheless a genuine attempt is made to admire and extol everything that has a real existence and to understand its meaning and purpose. If a man's greatness is to be estimated in terms of his influence on subsequent ages, then Plato's place is secure, and we shall not find a greater name in the ancient or the modern world.

CHAPTER XX

THE PHILOSOPHY OF ARISTOTLE
(384–322 B.C.)

PLATO AND ARISTOTLE

Two men find themselves in a small camp on a mountain side. There is a difference of opinion: one of them wants to press on to the summit, while the other wants to see what is happening at the foot of the mountain. When they look up, there is nothing but cloud, when they look down, there are only vague shapes and images in the village at the foot of the mountain. They agree to differ: one moves up to the heights of speculation and the other moves down to practical realities. The first is Plato, the second Aristotle.

Yet we must not exaggerate the difference between them. After all, they are both on the same mountain, and both interested in the same things. Both are seekers after Truth; it is just that one of them is content to view it from afar while the other is not satisfied till he can get to grips with it at close quarters. Sometimes they are said to represent diametrically opposed tendencies of the human mind, the mystical and the practical, abstract speculation and concrete experience, poetical faith and sceptical analysis, yet this is to misunderstand the position. History and tradition have unfairly sharpened the difference between them; in fact they have the same interests, face the same sets of facts, ask the same questions; the real difference lies in the methods they adopt of dealing with their data. Plato writes about life as if it were a great drama, Aristotle writes crisp, clever, feature articles about special subjects. The one does not exclude the other, but it is important to understand what they are doing in order to appreciate their methods and their discoveries.

Aristotle is very much like a radiologist. He is dealing with a real person and he has to find out the facts. In order to find the cause of the trouble he does not stand like a lighthouse-keeper shining his light across the bay in the hope that as it revolves it may by chance reveal something unusual. Aristotle has his patient on the machine and focuses his light on the cause of the trouble.

163

THE FACT-FINDER

This brings us to an important part of Aristotle's method: he looks for the whole moral world *within*. It is no use looking from a distance, just as it is futile to look only on external action. He looks on the world within, and leaves the world above to Plato.

But he also deals with individuals and is not much interested in impersonal groups. He does not try to take an X-ray picture of twenty individuals but of one. In the same way, when Aristotle spotlights an instinct or an impulse, he takes it by itself and tries to find out its nature and function. But at the end of the process, he has discovered something; he may not have solved the problem but at least he has found the cause of it, and this is an important stage in solving it.

But this must be carried a step farther: supposing our radiologist finds that the patient has a fractured rib and this is revealed on the picture in a certain way. He will assume that other fractured ribs which will come to his notice in the future can be detected by the method he has applied in the case of the first. He knows the way in which this particular fracture was revealed, and as other fractures may reasonably be expected to follow the same pattern, they may be classified. Facts that apply to one may apply to all, and this is what Aristotle means by finding out the 'form' or 'essence' of an object. It really means that sufficient is known about it to classify it. In describing his method we have been using a metaphor which Aristotle could not have used, but in disclosing how he applied his method, we must allow him to use his own metaphor.

As we have discovered, he believed that substantial being was in individual objects and not in mere universals. The purpose of philosophy was to discover the causes of these individual substances. In order that anything, say a statue, may come to be, four things are required:

(a) There must be the matter out of which it arises, e.g. a marble block.

(b) There must be an external principle of motion that starts the process of change, e.g. the mind, hand and tool of the sculptor.

(c) The form realized in and through this process, e.g. the form of the Phidian Zeus.

(d) There must be an end and an aim of the process and that is the complete statue as the goal of the sculptor's work.

From this illustration we may understand what Aristotle means when he says that in order for anything to come into being it must have a material, an efficient, a formal and a final cause.

INSTINCT AND REASON

A life that is governed solely by the impulses of nature is not the highest kind of life. Only a life that is governed by Reason will result

in true character. Aristotle's opinion is that man is an animal with a
mind. That is to say: in seeking to produce moral character two things
are necessary: instinctive impulse and rational election. This means
that either a man obeys his instincts or his mind. Instinct supplies
power, and rational election regulates the power. The former by itself
would produce unmoral animals, while the latter by itself would lead
to unmoral intelligences. One of Plato's parables will help to clarify
the point. He considers human personality to be a chariot drawn by
horses. Two things are possible: if all the horses pull in different
direction the chariot will be brought to a standstill. If one horse proves
more power than all the others, it will probably bring destruction upon
all. But this is to reckon without the charioteer. It is his job to control
the reins and guide the horses. Part of his job is to see that they run
at the same pace—to unify their energies. The horses represent
impulses and the charioteer represents reason. If there is to be any
integration in human personality reason must be in control.

MAN AND SOCIETY

This should not be regarded as simply an academic question, reason
must control human life not only for the good of the individual but for
the good of the community. Just as reason is necessary to govern
impulses, so government is necessary to the City-State. The secret of
good government is to create those conditions in which the good life
is attainable. The good life is possible only in contact with other lives.
Aristotle could not see any problem out of its context, and as far as
he was concerned its context was the polis. Man's true nature is seen
when he plays his full part in the life of the polis. This enables him
to realize his responsibilities, to develop his capacities and to recognize
his dependence upon others. In Aristotle's words: "He who is unable
to live in society, or who has no need because he is sufficient for himself, must either be a god or a beast."

The question arises however as to whether man is related only to
other men or to someone else who transcends all human beings. Is
goodness dependent on material possessions or are there deeper needs
of the soul which require satisfaction? In a fragment of one of his
dialogues Aristotle gives the answer: "Be assured that the good of
man does not depend upon the abundance of possessions, but upon the
right inner quality. Not even the body is regarded as in a happy condition, merely because it is decked out in resplendent robes, but only
if, though wanting in finery, it is well developed and in good health.
Likewise one should call only that man fortunate whose soul is ethically
developed rather than the man who is rich in outward possessions and

is worth nothing in himself. Even a horse is judged by its actual virtues. If it is a poor horse, it is not rated higher because it has a gold bit in its mouth and a costly harness on its back."

THE CHIEF GOOD FOR MAN

Aristotle was not very thrilled with the Platonic 'Idea' which seemed to be so far above the grasp of man. He wanted something within man's reach, and looked at life from the human rather than the divine side. He wrote: "Even if there is some one good which is universally predictable of goods or is capable of separate or independent existence, clearly it could not be achieved or attained by man; but we are now seeking something attainable." What did Aristotle mean by the particularity of goods?

It is possible for someone to give us a vivid description of a land beyond the summit of Everest, telling us of the rigours of the climate the remoteness from the rest of the world, the Buddhist monasteries and the search for the Lama, the people and their customs, the labours of the yak and the distresses under a foreign power, but the picture would be so general as to be imprecise, vague and inadequate. Aristotle's method would have been to frame and epitomize this vast scene by presenting the picture of a Tibetan. The rest of the picture would have to be built around this one figure. Aristotle used to particularize a thing, then analyse it, and then explain it. To put the matter in another way, the doctor is not concerned with 'good' in general or even 'good' in itself, but with the health of man, and the health of a particular man. In short, it is individuals that he is healing.

He looked for some specific form of human goodness and believed that this end was attainable by the good citizen of the Hellenic polis within the compass of his earthly life. The chief end of man was felicity and this was to be attained by:

(a) Exercising a right judgment in all things.

(b) Sharing the aims as well as the happiness of life in a community.

(c) Making his full contribution to the life and success of the City.

He emphasizes the typical Greek doctrine of the 'mean'—nothing in excess. Moderation was the philosophical guide of life for many Greeks. It stipulated that man must find the mean between two extremes, between knowing and doing, between the theoretical and practical, between potentiality and actuality, between the Chief Good and particular goods, and that felicity was to be found only in this principle of moderation. Aristotle also believed that some slaves and some non-Greeks did not possess the capacity for doing this, but he was a philosopher and not a moralist and perhaps may be excused for this odd opinion.

A GOD WHO IS REMOTE

Aristotle's interpreters have laid more stress on the First Cause, the Prime Mover, the unmoved Mover, than did Aristotle himself. The time factor can be omitted, for God is beyond time. Aristotle's concern was not that the process began at sometime, he was interested in the fact that it continued to function. The universe functioned now by the very same power that had always inspired and dynamized it. Underlying existence there is a life principle which begins, moves, changes, and concludes all things. It is not a question of who moved first, it is a question of who communicates life to all things. Although Aristotle criticizes Plato for his transcendentalism, he is guilty of it himself in that he cannot bring himself to place God within the world. God controls and moves all things but he does this from the outside. The line the train shall take is not decided by the driver but by the man in the signal box. Certainly there is something mechanical about this kind of external and remote control, but that is because there is something mechanical about Aristotle's doctrine of God.

He is not concerned about the character of God, and this is because he was not very interested in the character of man. His interest in human life is secondary, for the way a man lives is less important than how he thinks. In fact, the supreme business of life is the scientific contemplation of the physical world. Morality is useful because it enables man to make just and fair estimates of the working of the natural world. Study, for Aristotle, is more important than character. He was not interested in producing saints or prophets or heroes, but academics.

A GOD WHO IS UNKNOWN

Because he is concerned with academics, his view of God is limited to helping man to think correctly. But this is hardly befitting the function of a god. The character of God seems to be a side-issue, for he is brought in at the last moment, so to speak, to provide initiative for the physical movement of the world. St. Paul's reference to the unknown God must have been amply justified. Aristotle virtually reduces God to a mechanical toy. God pulls the signal but has neither the knowledge nor interest about what happens to the train. Nor does this matter as long as God does what he is supposed to do so that the universe keeps going. It follows that the universe fulfils its function, and finds its satisfaction in its endless revolutions, and the only connection between God and the world is the impersonal, detached, almost automatic signalman.

A further fact may be added: this celestial signalman will bring all the trains into the sidings in the end, for everything must be brought to its proper place. For Aristotle believed in that "far-off divine event to which the whole creation moves." God is like a magnet who draws all things to himself, and although this sounds like the doctrine of the happy ending, yet perhaps Aristotle thought that such a doctrine was necessary in order to compensate for the absence of any real hope of personal immortality. At least he did not hold out the hope of eternal life as a motive for good conduct in this life. His interest was not so much in the fact of an immortal destiny as in the contemplation of it.

Aristotle emphasizes the worthwhileness of this world and the essential goodness of all that exists. For many Greeks, matter was regarded as evil and therefore their lives and doctrines were shrouded in pessimism. Aristotle is the exception. Buddha had said the world was unreal; the Gnostics said the world was evil; Aristotle would have none of it. The Gnostics later repudiated some aspects of the Christian Faith, for they could not believe that God would lower himself by taking a material body, for matter was evil. If this is the case, morality has no meaning because man cannot help his material existence. Aristotle's belief in the essential goodness of the world was at once more refreshing and encouraging than the prevailing pessimism.

His emphasis on contemplation was to enable men to come to the right conclusions and one of his great achievements was to replace superstition by sound logic. Alongside this was his strong emphasis on the power of the individual mind.

But he was not free from criticism. Many old doctrines continued to hold sway and their adherents did not easily let go their beliefs. False beliefs in astrology still lingered and many believed that the stars were personal beings governing human lives. Aristotle's opposition to this theory was not well received. Also there lingered the popular belief in the existence of a racial mind, that the whole of the human race is united by this one mind.Aristotle's doctrine of particularity and of the power of the individual mind did much to explode such a theory. In the sense that he was concerned with the doctrine of being, with man's Chief Good, and with the whole question of the continuation of the universe, it may be said that his revolution was really religious. It was an appeal to Reason and to the authority of the senses. The range of subjects which he covered, his incisive mind, his clarity of thought, his daring pronouncements and his logical consistency, all combine to secure him a place among the great ones of our race.

CHAPTER XXI

CYNICS, STOICS AND EPICUREANS

DIOGENES 412–330 B.C.

The Cynics were mystics rather than philosophers, and their mysticism was of a very practical kind. Theirs was a revolt against accepted patterns of behaviour. There were no half-measures; what they believed had to be applied, and their beliefs were very unconventional. Many things were rejected outright: knowledge that did not end in virtue was useless; Platonic abstractions which were the product of the imagination were rejected; social conventions which continued to be a heavy drag on man's life were spurned, and the martial spirit, which inevitably brought out man's baser instincts, was anathema. The Cynics called for a return to simplicity, to nature, and to the way of non-violence. Although their founder was Antisthenes, the best known and the greatest of them was Diogenes (412–330). Mahatma Gandhi, going from place to place, wearing a simple dhoti and carrying a staff, was a sort of modern Diogenes. Indeed the comparison may be pressed further. Gandhi avoided physical pleasures, despised the conventions of society, and adopted a simple and natural life. In every respect he was following in the steps of Diogenes.

Back to Simplicity. The Cynics were concerned with moral conduct rather than philosophy, more interested in a way of life than in theories about it. It was their view that the world was getting too involved and complicated, and philosophy was blamed for this. The gracious influences of life were being passed by: gentleness, sensitivity and spirituality were being more and more ignored. Cynicism was a strong protest against these tendencies. They had little time for such matters as logic and physics because those subjects were remote and had little bearing on everyday life. Also Diogenes was impatient of Plato's speculative theories and took his stand with the disciple Thomas: "Unless I see I will not believe." Notice how the Realism of Diogenes is set up against the Idealism of Plato: "I can see a table, I cannot see Tabularity. I know Athens and Corinth and other cities and can see that they are all bad. As for the Ideal Society, show it me and I will say what I think."

All the external trimmings of life were regarded as of no value—
only Goodness was worth the effort of mind and will. Military honours,
civic rewards, titles, honorifics, riches—all these were mere toys lightly
to be cast aside, no more than empty supersititions. Here was a genuine
attempt to free human life from the external props on which it had
rested—money, matrimony, the social conventions and the approval
of others. The love of money was the cause of crime, war and worry;
poverty was not only the simplest but the happiest solution. Aphrodite
was no favourite of Diogenes and sometimes he threatened to shoot
her. Love was a curse and should be eradicated. Marriage multiplied
difficulties such as security, home-building, education of children, and
many other things, and therefore was to be discouraged.

Back to Nature. The word Cynic means 'dog-like,' and this was
their declared aim, to be like dogs. At its best there is much to commend this point of view, but at its worst it is little more than philosophic savagery, extremist, indecent and undesirable. A dog has no
inhibitions, no social obligations, no home, no possessions, no theories,
and according to Diogenes, that was the ideal sort of life. On the other
hand, a dog was faithful, forgiving, friendly, rarely spiteful and always
loyal and brave. But to live a dog's life may also involve being flea-
ridden, indecent and savage, and it must be confessed that the Cynics
could not be entirely exonerated in this respect. Careless of personal
appearance, sometimes dirty, and on occasion rude, they wandered
from place to place disregarding the customs of society and taking
pleasure in flouting those customs and offending the susceptibilities of
others.

Back to Non-violence. The Cynics were convinced that war and
crime had taken control of mankind. How did they counteract these
tendencies? If you possess little, there is no need to fight to defend it.
If you have no home, it doesn't matter very much who rules your
country. Diogenes would never retaliate. A workman carrying a pole
accidentally hit him and cried, "Look out!" "Why," said Diogenes,
"are you going to hit me again?"

The Cynics renounced political life lest it should bring them into
conflict with others. They attacked slavery because it involved cruelty.
In any case the difference between man and man was not based on
status but on moral values. To sum it up: fear nothing, desire nothing,
possess nothing, and happiness will follow.

The teaching of the Cynics was soon to be eclipsed by that of the
Stoics and Epicureans, yet the credit for blatantly opposing traditional
standards must go to Diogenes. Modifications of Cynic doctrine
appeared later but no one was quite as fearless, shocking and con-

sistent as Diogenes. In true Socratic fashion, he brought home to men forgotten truths and introduced many new ones. But the Stoics almost ignored Diogenes and soon put Plato again on the throne of philosophy.

ZENO (340–265 B.C.)

Zeno, the founder of Stoicism, was a native of Cyprus although much of his propaganda work was done at Rome. He set out to prove that the power operative in the universe was both rational and beneficent.

The Divine Reason. There was universal belief in certain overruling powers in the world, and this belief was strengthened by the passing ages. Men of all nations seem to have engraved on their minds the fact that their lives were under the control of divine power. More often than not the Greeks thought of divine powers rather than power. They pointed to the manifestations which the gods themselves had given; it was said that in the Battle of Regillus, Castor and Pollux were seen on horseback, fighting among the ranks of men. They also pointed to prophecy and divination, for if anyone interprets the will of a person, that person must exist.

The Stoics added other arguments which, it should be remembered, were not well known at that time. The musical harmony of the world would be impossible if there were no mind behind it. The sheer perfection of the natural world presupposes a Creator. Wordsworth was expressing a Stoic idea when he wrote: "A motion and a spirit that impels all thinking things, all objects of all thought, and moves through all things." A magnificent house presupposes an architect, so does a magnificent world. The motions of the sun, the moon, and the five planets are the work of an infinite mind. We see the world as the creation of Divine Providence, and realize that it was brought into being not by chance and accident but by Reason.

The Stoics were impressed by the agreement and sympathy, the affinity and inter-connection between all things. This underlying, inter-connecting link was Reason. Because the tree is protected by bark, and the vine has its tendrils, and animals reproduce their own kind, the Stoics held that all things were made for creatures possessing Reason.

Of course there is more in the world than order, beauty and design, so what was the Stoic reaction to the presence of evil? The power of evil was grossly underestimated by the Stoics and no doubt this is why they are able to offer only an ethic and not a Gospel. Man must learn by discipline and endurance to accept evil since he can do nothing about it. He has to learn to live with suffering, so he must rely on his own courage:

> Under the bludgeonings of chance
> My head is bloody but unbowed.

And he must also rely on the fact that the Divine Reason is indestructible. In the life of man, whatever is, is reasonable, and because it is reasonable, he should be content to accept it. If life is hard and demanding, it is his duty to face it. Moreover the Divine Reason is like a suit of armour covering a man, and when he is wearing this, the slings and arrows of outrageous fortune will have no power to hurt him.

In any case, the Stoic could sit lightly to the pains and woes of earthly life because he was buttressed by two great facts: his inner awareness of the Divine Reason, and the strength of his will. This enabled him not only to endure life's woes but to endure them and sing. Epictetus, the Greek Stoic writes:

"What else can I do, a lame old man, but sing hymns to God? If I were a nightingale, I would do the nightingale's part; if I were a swan, I would do as a swan. But now I am a rational creature, and I ought to praise God: this is my work; I do it, nor will I desert my post, so long as I am allowed to keep it. And I exhort you to join me in this same song."

Grades of Being. Although Reason pervades all things it does not indwell all creatures in the same degree. There are graduated stages of being. There is the vegetable kingdom which nature preserves by nurture and growth. A flower opens its petals to the sun and closes them at night, and the stalks of corn sway with the wind without breaking. Then there exists the animal kingdom where there are sensations, motives and appetites, the impulse to choose what is helpful and to avoid what is harmful. But to man is given Reason to control his appetites. By keeping unfettered that godlike element, man is able to live an upright life. This means that man need never be afraid. "You are part of God Himself," said Epictetus, and this thought banishes fear. It also has a profound effect on a man's character. It was the Stoic faith which enabled Marcus Aurelius to say: "Others pray: let me be done with that man! Do thou, Marcus, pray: Let me not wish to be done with him! Others: Let me not lose my little child! Thou: Let me not fear to lose him! In short, pray in this spirit and await the outcome."

The forth scale of being consists of the good and wise who possess perfect and absolute reason, and this can only refer to the gods themselves. On the whole, however, the Stoics spoke less of the gods than of God and the Divine Reason. The following utterance of Seneca is typical: "We worship and adore the framer and former of the universe;

not the happiness which results from the gratification of desire. In fact, he had much in common with Gotama. Both were oppressed by the sorrows and evils of life; both sought a way of emancipation; both sought it through meditation, and both found it in a blissful experience which one called Nirvana and the other Happiness. Epicurus set out to find a way of freedom from want, from fear and superstition, and from illusion.

Freedom from want. The background of their lives was altogether dissimilar. The Buddha, as we have seen, was born in a royal household, but Epicurus was made a helpless refugee when he was a boy in his teens. The King of Thrace attacked Samos and the Athenian colonists had to flee to Colophon. This disaster meant that the family could not send Epicurus to the School of Philosophy to continue his studies, so he had no option but to settle down to face and try to solve the problems which surrounded him. It was a hard school but it had one important result, it meant that Epicureanism was the outcome of a man's reflections on his own experience. His philosophy had come through the fires of conflict and deprivation. He suffered all the disadvantages of refugee life—poverty, discomfort, loneliness and a sense of frustration. This brought home to him the value of affection and friendship. He discovered that the companionship of like-minded souls was a strong fortress against the cruelties of the world. In those circumstances courage also was a necessity, and in that respect he was the finest example of his message. Justice was the great bulwark against the evils which men bring upon one another, and to believe in Justice, even when it appears to be disregarded by others, was an antidote to all kinds of evil. There is an element of indifferentism in this, but it must be remembered that he was the victim of a callous and unjust society, and sometimes he had to take refuge in his idealistic dreams. It is to his credit that there is no note of cynicism in his message.

Freedom from fear. What was the cause of the sort of situation in which he and his fellow refugees found themselves? They were a little company of victimized, fearful creatures and Epicurus had to find some means of solace for them. He came to the conclusion that unjustifiable fears surrounded their lives: they were afraid of the next move of their conquerors; they were afraid of the gods who seemed to be hostile to them, and they were afraid of death. Fear was the great demon and it must be cast out. This could be done only by meditation on life's joys, for the pleasures of the mind were more rewarding and lasting than the pleasures of the senses. Happiness, not fear, was the goal of life. Nor should they fear the gods for the gods were not concerned about them. The gods, it appeared, had been too weak to protect them against life's evils so the best thing to do was to ignore them and find some way of escape. Death was a dreamless sleep, a passing into oblivion, and there was no reason to fear it. There may be some limitations in the reasoning of Epicurus but at least he is not indulging in idle speculations. He was facing a practical situation with its accompanying problems, and this fact gave an urgency and an intensity to his message which are not to be found in the more objective musings of Zeno.

Freedom from illusion. Epicurus had been influenced by Democritus the Atomist, that is to say he believed that all things could be reduced to minute particles of different shape—atoms. There are many things that are no more than appearances or illusions and it is important not to be misled by these. Basically there are only atoms and the void. This has important consequences: it means that all things happen by mechanical necessity. Although this savours of fatalism, it is surely preferable to the view that all the calamities which had befallen the wretched refugees had been due to chance and accident. But Epicurus was saved from fatalism by the view that the human spirit and will had the power to triumph over necessity in the end.

It was a down-to-earth philosophy, materialistic and empirical. But its founder was facing harsh realities and practical problems. Nevertheless the keynote of his message was moderation. He taught his people to find a happy medium between extremes. They should not expect too much from life and then they would not be disillusioned. They should seek happiness as the goal, yet should not be too disappointed if it eluded them. They should avoid sorrow and suffering, but if they were brought to the test, they should face it with courage and without bitterness.

Lucretius looked upon Epicurus as the prophet and saviour of mankind:

> *He passed behind*
> *The world's last flaming wall, and through the whole*
> *Of space unchartered ranged his mind and soul.*
> *Whence, conquering, he returned to make Man see*
> *At last what can, what cannot, come to be;*
> *By what law to each Thing its power hath been*
> *Assigned, and what deep boundary set between;*
> *Till underfoot is tamed Religion trod,*
> *And by his victory, Man ascends to God.*

This is a fine tribute but the poet's imagination just oversteps the bounds of truth, for Epicurus was not really concerned about Man ascending to God, he was concerned to show Man's self-sufficiency. His aim was to throw Man back upon his own resources, independently of God. He believed that Man had been crushed by the burden of

Religion and must be set free to work out his own salvation. Nevertheless, Epicurus has provided the finest expression of Humanism ever penned.

Why did he win many followers ? Because his teaching was reasonable and convincing; because he not only stated his doctrine but followed it himself; because he lived simply, almost ascetically; because the message of Affection and Friendship was like a soothing balm to men and women crushed by the injustices of a tyrannous world. But the main reason for the success of his work was that it proved effective in the lives of ordinary people. In times of social unrest and disaster his words brought new strength and new hope, and thereby lifted the lives of men on to a higher plane.

CHAPTER XXII

THE MYSTERY RELIGIONS

SEVERAL Mystery Cults were in vogue in the Roman world at the time of the Advent of Christ—these were the cults of Mithra, Cybele, Serapis, the Eleusinian Mysteries, and the Delphic Oracle. By far the most important of these was the first and this we shall consider in some detail.

MITHRA IN PERSIAN WORSHIP

A passing reference was made to Mithra in the chapter on Persian religion, but Persia by no means exhausts the history of this remarkable cult. In the Avesta we find a triad composed of Ahura, Mithra, and Anahita. Ahura is the Lord of Wisdom, Mithra the Lord of Light, and Anahita the Goddess of Fertility or the Unblemished One. Strabo says: "They (the Persians) honour also the Sun whom they call Mithra, and the Moon, and Aphrodite, and Fire and Earth, and Winds and Water." Aphrodite was the Greek name for Anahita. Mithra and Anahita are closely linked together and sometimes a bull was sacrificed in their honour.

Mithra also has a place in the Persian judgment scene. Ahura presided over the court of justice, but a trinity of judges, acting in obedience to the will of Ahura, gave the decisions. These were Mithra, Sraosha and Rashnu. Rashnu holds the scales of destiny, while Sraosha represents Obedience, and Mithra, Purification. Mithra guards the entrance to the Other World. Although Zoroaster concentrates his attention on Ahura and completely ignores Mithra, the Avesta pays reverence to Ahura and Mithra as gods of like power.

Mithra had other functions too; he was the god of contracts and covenants, both making them and enabling others to keep them. He gave victory in time of war and helped the righteous into Paradise. He was also regarded as the benefactor of men by slaying the primeval Bull.

MITRA IN INDIAN WORSHIP

After the Aryan migration to India three gods soon became prominent: Varuna, the all-seeing god and the judge of men; Indra, the god who provided the rains, and Mitra, the Sun-god. There is in the Vedas an invocation to the rising Sun which is believed to be the essence of Vedic worship.

May we meditate on that excellent glory of the Sun-god:
May he prosper our meditations.

Another feature of Mitra worship is that it was said to burn away uncleanness.

"O Sun, burn up my deeds of the night—sins of thought, word or deed, committed by the hand, foot, stomach or the senses. I throw all these into the sacrificial fire, which is lit in our hearts that they may be burnt up."

Mithra is another name for 'friend' and this inspires his worshippers with thoughts of benevolence: "May all the world be happy, may they be healthy, may they be comfortable and never miserable. May the rain come down in the proper time and may the earth yield plenty of grain." There is kindliness in such a prayer even if it is not petition of the most spiritual order.

By 200 B.C. the Vedic gods were still recognized in India but they were less powerful and less popular than previously, and with the ever increasing prestige of Brahma, Siva and Vishnu, not much is heard of Mitra and the rest.

MITHRA IN ROMAN WORSHIP

While Mitra was fading into obscurity in India, his star was in the ascendant in the Roman World, and devotees were being won throughout the far-flung empire. There now takes place an unexpected turn of events which was to make the forgotten Persian Mithra and the waning Indian Mitra the most popular object of worship in the Greco-Roman world. Mithra was introduced to Rome in 67 B.C. by Pompey's captives from Asia Minor. There were several reasons why Mithraism gained momentum in the new empire.

Reasons for its popularity. Doubtless Greek influence was very strong but Platonic teaching was too remote and complicated for the Roman soldiery. The principles of Stoicism were all very well for rare souls like Seneca and Aurelius with their philosophic training but they were not easily understood by the ordinary man. It is true that Emperor worship was gaining prominence, but this was not only a compulsory religion, it was also denuded of any spiritual content. The Romans needed a Faith which would bring inspiration, strength and redemption, and these blessings they found in the worship of Mithra.

Mithraism was a man's religion. Only men were permitted to be initiated into its mysteries and it soon became a close brotherhood of men at arms. A worshipper of Mithra was expected to show many qualities such as endurance, strength and courage. The ancient Persians had believed that Mithra led them to victory and perhaps it was natural that such a god would appeal to men whose main interest in life was conquest. His official title also attracted them: he was Sol invictus Mithra, the unconquered Sun Mithra. He was the Sun who always conquered darkness and renewed his strength every morning. The assurance of resilience as he struggled against Barbarian darkness was a source of great inspiration to the Roman.

Mithra was also the god of oaths and covenants, and woe betide the man who broke an oath made under the seal of Mithra. But the god in whose name the oath was made also gave the power to keep it, and this was another reason for the soldier's dependence upon him. Every man was ultimately answerable to Mithra, the guardian of the covenants.

A Roman soldier's life was often short but glorious, and the thought of death was never far away. It was a great consolation to know, therefore, that Mithra stood at the entrance to Paradise, and although the Romans were renowned for their courage they would not lightly ignore the One who held the keys of the Other World.

There was an element of hero worship in the Mithraic cult, for while Mithra influenced the Romans and inspired them to superhuman feats of courage, they embellished the character of Mithra and elevated him to a Warrior God. It was sufficient for them that he had won the greatest victory in primeval times by slaying the sacred Bull. This was the warrior who feared no foe and who now symbolized eternal victory. He was the soldier's ideal, the prototype of the Roman spirit. Every man wanted to be as intrepid as the One who fearlessly drove the spear into the ferocious Bull. The conclusion is obvious: every aspect of Mithraism was calculated to appeal to the martial spirit of the proud and confident Roman.

If they were convinced devotees, they were also consistent missionaries. Just as the religion of Allah was diffused by the Muslim conquerors, so the cult of Mithra spread with the conquests of the Roman legionaries. Their efforts were aided by the fact that Mithra's name was already known in many lands, in Mesopotamia, Persia, India and Greece, and although the Romans added an elaborate ritual, they were proclaiming a god whose name and fame were well-known and revered. Inevitably they brought with them their religion when they conquered the Anglo-Saxons. Ironically it was the Romans themselves who were responsible for displacing Mithra in the affections of their new captives by introducing Christianity as well. Although there is evidence of Mithra chapels in some parts of Britain—in Colchester, London and York—these were mainly in Roman Army settlements, and there is little evidence that Mithraism was very popular among the Britons. Christianity's emphasis on reason, its ethical implications, its logical teaching, its impressive if less spectacular worship, appealed to the more reserved and placid minds of the Anglo-Saxons. In no Roman colony was Mithraism so coolly received as in Britain.

Mithraic ritual. The taurobolium was borrowed from the ritual of Cybele, the cult of the Great Mother. It represented the sacrifice of the sacred Bull which was offered to the Sun. The initiate stood under a grating while the blood of the slain bull flowed over him, redeeming him. This gory ceremony, so fascinating to some, was utterly repugnant to others.

Even in ancient Persia Mithra was a kind of mediator between Ahura and Ahriman, and this aspect was now emphasized by the Romans, except that Mithra was now the Mediator between the supreme God and mankind, and the devotees of Mithra were quick to stress this particular concept when Christianity came on the scene. In works of art Mithra is seen as a strong young man slaying the Bull on behalf of mankind. In addition to the dramatic initiation ceremony there were sacred feasts, not unlike the Christian Eucharist, stated times of prayer —dawn, noon and sunset, and perhaps it was the striking similarities to Christian ritual which made Mithraism a serious rival to Christianity for at least three centuries. Moreover, the birthday of Mithra was December 25th, and as Christianity gained ascendancy over its rival, it used the old festival day on which to celebrate the birthday of Christ. This alone was borrowed from Mithraism and by it we may judge both the importance and the downfall of the cult. But the adopting of the date was no accident, for it showed how completely Christianity had superseded Mithraism, and by Christianizing a festival dear to the Romans it centred their attention on the central doctrine of the Incarnation and this helped to win the day.

The decline of Mithraism. Other factors contributed to this outcome, for, although the similarities were striking, they were superficial. Christ was an historical person, Mithra was not. Mithraism countenanced the traditional gods of Rome, Christianity did not. Mithraism was limited to men and to a particular type of man, in Christ there was neither male nor female, bond nor free. It is hardly possible that a religion could hope to succeed which disregarded the more religious and more numerous section of the race. But there was a deeper reason: there was in the Roman character a hard, intractable, cruel streak, and this was revealed in their attitude to children, especially the crippled, to their slaves, and to women, and more especially, to their enemies, among whom were the Christians. Their insatiable blood-lust was partly satisfied by visits to the gladiatorial arena, and everyone knows that when there was a large number of Christians to be thrown to the lions, Nero would offer his gardens for the spectacle. In the end, a religion must be judged by its fruits, and the ethical consequences of Mithraism were hard to find. A religion should give to human life gentleness as well as strength, compassion as well as courage, concern for others as well as confidence, and the real defect of Mithraism was that it seemed to emphasize the so-called masculine virtues while leaving the others untouched.

In addition to this, the world had grown weary of 'the boast of heraldry and the pomp of power' and cried out for something simple, clean, wholesome and constructive. People were no longer interested in the blood baths, the marching feet, the glint of steel, the flashing spear of Mithra, and they looked eagerly and wistfully for something else. The fact is, the mood of the world had changed. It was not simply a change of thought, it was the desire for a change of heart. The awakened conscience, the conviction of sin, thoughts of penitence, and the desire for the good life, all these were signs of the change of mood. Caesar's image of power was to be replaced by an image of love, for there was soon to appear on the scene one whose purpose Mithra, Cybele and Serapis had no power to thwart and whose progress could not be stayed. This new image—the gentle, compassionate Nazarene—changed the beliefs as well as the thoughts of men, and under the impact of His presence the traditional gods of Rome like the Olympian gods of Greece vanished into oblivion.

THE CULT OF SERAPIS

Although Mithraism was the most serious rival of the Christian Faith, that is not to say that the others could be ignored. In the case of all the mystery cults an ancient god was given a more virile and resplendent form. The cult of Serapis was a revival of Egyptian Osirian worship. The word Serapis is formed from Osiris-Apis. In common with other mystery cults its initiates took vows of secrecy about the rites and teachings of the cult. Whereas Osiris had been the consort of Isis in Egypt, as well as her brother and husband, Serapis became her consort in the Roman Empire. Although it is often referred to as the cult of Serapis, the ritual connected with it shows that it is really a revival of the cult of Isis. Isis was at once a fertility goddess and an ideal Mother. In Egypt she was the corn goddess and grains of corn were offered in worship. Since she was also believed to have discovered wheat and barley, her title as fertility goddess was not misplaced.

In Rome she was worshipped as the ideal Mother and the pictures of her suckling the infant Horus are very similar to those of the Madonna and Child. As she had been the ideal wife of Osiris in Egypt, she became the ideal wife of Serapis in Rome. Naturally she appealed especially to Roman women who were shocked by the blood-thirsty and licentious rites connected with other Oriental cults. It was, however, the Greeks and not the Egyptians or Romans, who ascribed to her another honour—that of deity of mariners, and Sirius, the bright star of Isis, received its name from her. It follows that she was a fertility goddess, an ideal Wife and Mother, as well as a guiding star for mariners. But the adherents of the Serapis cult were most interested in her power to bestow immortality. Here again her Egyptian origin is noticeable. In Egypt she had been aided by many other deities in her search for the body of Osiris. Eventually she found it and restored it to life, so the cult really deals with the death and resurrection of a divine being. Those who were initiated into its secret rites and worshipped Serapis and Isis were assured that they, like Osiris, would triumph over death. It was this hope of the life to come that greatly interested the Romans and many of the Emperors were among her most devoted worshippers. This worship was similar to that of other mystery cults: times of prayer and fasting, bathing in sacred water (a relic of its association with the Nile), and the waiting for the appearance of Serapis. The cult is less important for its ceremonial than for its marked impact on Roman life. It did three things for the people of Rome which other cults failed to do: it sanctified family life and gave it new ideals, it emphasized the gentle virtues— patience, faithfulness and compassion, and gave an assurance of the life to come.

THE CULT OF CYBELE

This cult is more extraordinary, sensational and barbaric than those already mentioned. The reason why it was introduced to Rome was a strictly utilitarian one. The story begins with the rise of Hannibal, the great Carthaginian ruler whose father made him swear at the altar eternal hatred of the Romans. By 204 B.C. he had already inflicted several serious defeats on Roman armies, and the rumour spread that only the goddess Cybele, of Phrygian origin, could deliver them from the mighty Hannibal. Therefore, the small black stone which was said to contain the divine power of Cybele was carried to Rome in 204 B.C. and placed in the temple of victory on the Palatine Hill. The fact that Hannibal was soon afterwards defeated by Scipio lent some credence to the popular view of Cybele's power. At any rate, her popularity increased and brought with it a sad deterioration in the Roman character.

The main purpose of its worship was to bring back to life Cybele's son, Attis. This could only be achieved when men surrendered their virility, and in consequence castration became a common practice in their ritual. The savage orgies on the Day of Blood made this one of the more unsavoury cults which Rome too easily adopted. Its savage ceremonies, its spectacular processions, its frenzied dances, and its all-important taurobolium appealed to those who craved for emotional stimulants and unnatural experiences. That it remained in vogue for four hundred years is less a tribute to its usefulness than an indictment of Roman society. All these cults were very popular for a time but their days were numbered. Mithra, Serapis and Cybele were soon to die never to rise again, and it was precisely this capacity to die and yet rise again as revealed in another Lord, which ultimately brought about their downfall.

REFERENCES

Page   Line

Part I

9   19   F. T. Palgrave, *The Golden Treasury* (Oxford University Press), p. 250.

12   28   G. L. May, ed., *English Religious Verse*, Shelley's "Adonis" (Everyman's Library), p. 164.

28   22   *Methodist Hymn Book* (London: The Epworth Press, Publishers), Hymn 539, stanza 1.

40   21   *Methodist Hymn Book*, Hymn 742, stanza 4.

41   15   F. W. H. Myers, *Saint Paul* (London: Simpkin & Marshall), p. 18.

45   22   Griffiths Translation. *Rigveda* (Benares), I.97.

49   4   *Methodist Hymn Book*, Hymn 513, stanza 1.

49   16   M. Wood, ed., *The Works of William Shakespeare* (Standard Literature), p. 104.

57   28   Griffiths Translation. *Rigveda*, X.90.

62   14   R. E. Hume, ed., *Thirteen Principal Upanishads* (New York and London: Oxford University Press), Svetas 307.

62   35   W. Wordsworth, Preface to *The Excursion* (Everyman's Library).

63   6   *Methodist Hymn Book*, Hymn 742, stanza 2.

65   26   Griffiths Translation. *Rigveda*, X.129.

65   30   *Ibid.*, X.121.

Part II

79   24   *Methodist Hymn Book*, Hymn 72, stanza 5.

83   9   J. B. Pritchard, ed., *Ancient Near Eastern Texts* (Princeton University Press), p. 100.

89   32   J. Addison, *Portius*. Act I, Scene 2.

92   2   *The Works of R. W. Emerson* (London: Routledge's Popular Library), p. 1.

Page	Line	
92	13	W. S. Churchill, *Great Contemporaries* (London: Macmillan & Co., Ltd., 1937), p. 13.
96	33	H. B. Cotterill, tr., *The Odyssey*, Book VIII.
97	29	W. G. De Burgh, *The Legacy of the Ancient World* (Barnes & Noble, Inc., 1960), p. 112.
99	12	Stephen Neill, *Christian Faith To-day* (Pelican Books), p. 55.
102	13	Greek Anthology, Dionysius.
102	28	Greek Anthology, Seneca.
103	43	G. Murray, *Five Stages of Greek Religion*, p. 72.
118	20	A. Domet, "Christmas Hymn." See *Oxford Dictionary of Quotations*, p. 184.

PART III

132	8	A. Erman, *The Religion of Egypt*, p. 107.
133	26	C. Marston, *The Bible Comes Alive* (London: Eyre & Spottiswoode, Ltd.), pp. 59–60.
139	25	Griffths Translation. *Rigveda*, I.164.
141	36	J. H. Moulton, *The Treasure of the Magi* (London: Oxford University Press), pp. 162–163.
148	36	*Buddhist Hymns* (Colombo).
149	10	H. C. Warren, *Buddhism in Translations*, p. 146.
151	6	Davids Rys, *Psalms of the Sutra*, Canto 26.
151	13	*Buddhist Hymns*.
157	13	S. T. Coleridge, "Self-knowledge," in *Poems*, p. 380.
161	23	*Hymns Ancient & Modern*, Hymn 573, stanza 3.
172	3	F. T. Palgrave, *The Golden Treasury*, "Invictus," by W. E. Henley, p. 476.
176	29	G. Murray, *Five Stages of Greek Religion*, p. 107.

SUGGESTIONS FOR FURTHER READING

PART I

Breasted, J. H., *The Conquest of Civilization*. Harper & Brothers 1926.

Frankfort, H., and others, *Before Philosophy*. Penguin Books, Ltd., 1959.

Howells, W., *Man in the Beginning*. London: G. Bell & Sons, Ltd.

James, Edwin O., *Beginnings of Religion*. Hillary House, Inc.

James, Edwin O., *The Social Function of Religion*. London: Hodder & Stoughton, Ltd., 1940.

Jevons, Frank B., *The Idea of God in Early Religion*. Cambridge University Press, 1910.

Marett, Robert R., *The Threshold of Religion*. London: Methuen & Co., Ltd.

Murphy, J., *The Origin and History of Religions*. Manchester University Publs.

Rivers, W. H. R., *Medicine, Magic and Religion*. International Library of Psychology.

Schmidt, W., *The Growth of Religion*. London.

Waterhouse, E. S., *The Dawn of Religion*. London: The Epworth Press, Publishers.

PART II

Bailey, Cyril (ed.), *Legacy of Rome*. Oxford University Press, 1923.

Bevan, Edwyn R. and Singer, C. J. (eds.), *Legacy of Israel*. London: Oxford University Press, 1927.

Childs, V. S., *New Light on the Most Ancient East*. Grove Press, 1957.

De Burgh, William G., *Legacy of the Ancient World*. Barnes & Noble, Inc., 1960.

Finegan, Jack, *Light from the Ancient Past*. Princeton University Press, 1946.

Glover, T. R., *The Ancient World*. Penguin Books, Ltd., 1945.

Hooke, S. H., *Babylonian and Assyrian Religion*. Oxford: Basil Blackwell & Mott, Ltd., 1953.

King, L. W., *Babylonian Legend and Mythology*. London.

Marston, C., *The Bible Comes Alive*. London: Eyre & Spottiswoode, Inc., 1950.

Parrott, A., *Discovering Buried Worlds*. London: SCM Press, Ltd.

PART III

Cornford, F. M., *Greek Religious Thought*. London.

Fowler, W. W., *The Religious Experience of the Roman People*. London: Gifford Leots.

Frankfort, H., *Ancient Egyptian Religion*. Columbia University Press, 1948.

Glanville, Stephen R. K. (ed.), *Legacy of Egypt*. London: Oxford University Press, 1942.

Guthrie, W. K. C., *The Greeks and Their Gods*. Beacon Press, Inc., 1955.

Joad, Cyril E. M., *Return to Philosophy*. Humanities Press, Inc.

Masani, Rustom, *Zoroastrianism: The Religion of the Good Life*. Collier Books, 1962.

Murray, George, *Five Stages of Greek Religion*. Doubleday & Company, Inc., 1913.

Murti, T. R. V., *The Central Philosophy of Buddhism*. The Macmillan Company, 1955.

Ward, C. H. S., *Buddhism*. London: The Epworth Press, Publishers.

Waterhouse, J. W., *Zoroastrianism*. London: The Epworth Press, Publishers.